GRIT & GRACE

A MOTHER'S STORY

SUDHEER, SHARATH, DEEPAK

Published by Genesis Consulting Services Pty Ltd
34, Cavendish Way, Parkwood WA 6147
Copyright © Deepak Daniel,

First published 2026
Self Published

ISBN: 978-1-7635190-4-6
Design & typesetting by AtriTeX Technologies Private Limited

DEDICATION

*To our incredible Mother, whose
unwavering grit forged a legacy of love,
dreams, and enduring strength.*

All of my days, I will sing of Your greatness
All of my days, I will speak of Your grace
All of my days, I will tell of Your wondrous love
Your love in Our life, Your love

by Mark Leslie Stevens

ACKNOWLEDGEMENTS

Writing *Grit and Grace* has been an emotional journey. It wasn't easy to revisit a life lived many years ago and give life to those feelings and experiences once more. While challenging, it was also a profound joy, and I did not undertake this journey alone.

I express my sincere gratitude to the Almighty for providing the strength to persevere and the voice to share these experiences. To my parents, my first teachers, I owe you everything. Your sacrifices and dedication shaped our lives, and your guidance instilled in me the importance of remembering our roots, regardless of where life takes us.

To my creative partners, Sudheer-Sheeba and Sharath-Smitha, I am grateful for your collaboration in bringing our vision to fruition. Your guidance refined these stories into their present form. To my beloved Asha, thank you for your unwavering support during long nights of writing and for your steadfast belief and encouragement. To my children, Alan and Ben, you are my greatest joy. I hope these stories inspire you to approach the world with courage and kindness.

I am deeply grateful to my extended family for your encouragement and for demonstrating that distance does not diminish the bonds of love. My uncles and aunts provided unwavering support, while my cousins helped me to be who I am. You are the community that keeps me grounded.

Finally, to the reader, thank you for allowing us to share our experiences. Whether you are in a bustling Indian city or a quiet suburb elsewhere, I hope you find resonance within these pages. I hope our "Mother's story" evokes meaningful emotions for you.

This book is dedicated to honoring the resilience of the human spirit particularly for those who pursue their dreams with grace.

Deepak Daniel

STORIES

CHAPTER 1

THE WORLD TURNED UPSIDE DOWN

The ring of my phone pierced the quiet of the ASB bank office in Auckland. It was approximately 11 a.m. on that challenging Friday, 30 June 2017. My uncle's voice on the other end was troubled and heavy as he said, "Your mother is unwell. She has been taken to the hospital. Will you be able to come?"

The news was not entirely unexpected, yet it carried a weight that no amount of preparation could ease. I had only recently returned to Auckland, six weeks prior, after spending over a month in Bangalore. As I sat in the quiet of my office, my mind drifted back to December 2016, when our entire family had gathered in India to stay with Mom for several weeks.

During that visit, she had mentioned persistent back pain. At the time, we checked with doctors, it was manageable and certainly not life-threatening. At sixty-nine, her doctors had dismissed the discomfort as a natural byproduct of age and the cumulative toll of a demanding, hardworking life. We had also grown accustomed to her physical limitations after her paralytic stroke in October 2007. Her right side was restricted, a challenge she met with her trademark quiet resilience.

I left for Auckland in the second week of January 2017, carrying with me the warmth of that time spent together. She had appeared well then, and those weeks now feel like an invaluable gift. We were completely unaware of the health challenges that were already gathering on the horizon.

Upon resuming work, I focused on establishing my reputation at the new company, having started in December 2016. Maintaining daily conversations with Mom remained a priority. Given the seven and a half hour time difference between New Zealand and India, I would speak with her each evening after work. This routine, built and nurtured over many years, gave us a special space to speak freely. We shared our moments of happiness and our struggles. We talked about plans, financial matters and even the occasional disagreements with my siblings. These conversations provided a vital connection to my roots.

My family and friends recognise that I am committed to maintaining and building relationships, though my approach had become more pragmatic and direct in recent years. Mom did not entirely approve of this change, although she understood it was my way. She often expressed concern about my future, fearing I might become isolated as I aged, and suggested that I was too aloof and insufficiently sensitive. As a result, our conversations frequently returned to this topic. She would often ask who the four people would be present at my passing. I was not particularly troubled by these discussions, believing that straightforwardness simplifies life and attracts genuine individuals.

Our conversations frequently centered on my relationships with my brothers, as well as various cousins, uncles, and aunts from both sides of the family. We shared a tendency to withdraw communication following disagreements, sometimes for days, both in my childhood and during her youth. This pattern occasionally persisted between us. While disagreements sometimes led to brief periods of silence, these intervals rarely lasted long. The longest such period was approximately a week during my university years, though my recollection is not precise.

After returning from India after a brief holiday in January 2017, our conversations became more subdued, likely due to the fluctuating intensity of her back pain. During her brief illness in October 2016, scans indicated her back pain was related to age-related hip joint pain, and treatment proceeded accordingly. In early March 2017, my brother Sharath, who lived in Bangalore with his wife Smitha and their son Alan, took her to Baptist Hospital. Mom had been living with Sharath since Asha, Ben, and I moved to Auckland. My youngest brother, Sudheer, and his wife, Sheeba, relocated to Hyderabad in 2013, the same year we moved to New Zealand. Baptist Hospital served as our family hospital, being the closest to our residence in Bangalore and employing several family members.

Since the pain was not reducing, doctors recommended further investigations. Blood sugar levels necessitated postponement of certain procedures. Subsequent scans revealed complications, though nothing was explicitly described as dangerous. Although Rani, my sister-in-law hinted at concerns and we reviewed the results, we still anticipated a normal outcome.

2017 At Aster hospital for investigation with my aunt Vasanthamma

Despite being busy with his work in construction, Sharath ensured that he took Mom to the hospital for regular check-ups. He had witnessed several fluctuations in her health. In fact, Mom had been quite unwell in 2016. She was admitted to hospital, and while there wasn't one specific ailment, her creatinine levels were concerning, she had an infection, and her health suddenly deteriorated. She was treated at Baptist Hospital, recovered within a week, and was back at home when we visited during Christmas 2016.

One of the subsequent scans revealed a form of kidney cancer. While the doctors initially did not describe it as serious, the finding nevertheless prompted a PET scan. On 30 March 2017, we received the PET scan report, which was devastating. She was diagnosed with stage 4 cancer that had metastasised. I was at work when I received this news, experiencing a mix of shock and desperate hope. Immediately after learning of her condition, the three of us travelled to India on 4 April. Sudheer and Sheeba also arrived in Bangalore. Witnessing her pain was deeply distressing. Although I sensed she knew her health was deteriorating, she was not fully aware of the extent. In India, doctors often communicate the gravity of a diagnosis to immediate family members rather than the patient, using phrases such as, "Please let your family members know," or "Take the patient home, perhaps they will be happier at home." Our emotional attachment often leads us to deny reality and make decisions driven by hope rather than logic. My aunt Vasanthamma, Mom's younger sister, shared that Mom had asked whether she would ever see me again after our Christmas visit in 2016. Mom's question suggested she sensed something was amiss. When I saw her again on 4 April, I reassured her that distance would not prevent me from visiting her when she wanted. We consulted doctors, sought second opinions, and explored all possible care options. One of the doctors at RL Jalappa Hospital, where my cousin Ananda worked, reviewed her reports and recommended surgery, suggesting that it was not a major issue and could potentially improve her quality of life for up to five years. This offered us hope, as previous consultations had not. Conversely, a doctor at Kidwai Hospital advised against excessive intervention, recommending that she be allowed to live without pain.

While all this was unfolding, Mom remained unaware of the gravity of her condition. Having worked in the health department herself, she knew something was wrong but couldn't diagnose it herself. One day, I sat with her and explained her condition without revealing its severity, telling her it was kidney cancer and that one of her kidneys would need to be removed. She didn't react strongly, asking only how straightforward the operation would be, perhaps knowing how difficult it could be, having undergone several major surgeries in the past. I felt like I was trying to mislead someone who had lived and worked in the medical field for over 40 years.

April 2017 before going to surgery, healthy and calm.

We mentally prepared ourselves for her surgery on the 20th of April. While she underwent a few chemotherapy sessions, they did not yield any positive results. In fact, during the chemotherapy, my mother struggled greatly, even the tablets didn't sit well with her, and she would vomit. She had lost weight, and her food intake had significantly decreased. Despite the physical toll, when we discussed the surgery with her, she accepted it with her characteristic quiet resolve. We didn't realise then that it was a decision that would not lead to her recovery. We stayed a few more days with Mom and returned when she appeared to be improving. The doctor had also mentioned that she might be all right for a few more years. I had booked to go back and see her in September and December of the same year.

Therefore, when I received the phone call, my initial assumption was that Mom was seriously unwell again. Approximately thirty minutes later, a friend from India called to offer condolences. I assured him, with confidence, that she was only unwell and that my brother had taken her to the hospital. Even as I spoke, my mind went blank, trying to make sense of what happened. I did not want him to be correct, so I asked how he had learned the news. He explained that my cousin Leena, who is my age and attended the same school, had shared the news of Mom's passing in a WhatsApp group for our classmates. I immediately ended the call, feeling devastated. My legs shook, my voice grew loud and incoherent, and my thoughts scattered. Overwhelmed by emotion, I felt helpless, thousands of miles away in my office, uncertain how to express my feelings or whom to approach. After a period of confusion and numbness, I called Prabhakar uncle, Mom's younger brother, to seek clarity. He responded indirectly, taking time to convey that she had lived a rich life and had now moved on to an eternal place.

It took a while for the news to sink in, that Mom was no longer with us. I had spoken to her only a few days earlier, though our conversations were brief due to her difficulty in speaking. When I approached my manager, Kate, I broke down in tears. A significant chapter of my life had ended. I had last seen Mom in May, and now she had joined my father, the love of her life.

I was unaware of the legacy Mom had left behind. We did not anticipate the difficulty of filling her role or the magnitude of the void her absence created. We had yet to realise the extent of her blessings, the pride we could feel, and the impact she had on her workplace, communities, friends, and family. Some stories highlight her resilience, while others reveal her grace. Through reflection, our family began to understand her life more deeply than ever before.

A. S. Jayamma was a mother, sister, cousin, friend, mother-in-law, grandmother, colleague, boss, and above all, a humble individual. A testament to grit and grace.

CHAPTER 2
THREE MUSKETEERS

The familiar hiss of the kerosene pump stove, sometimes sputtering before settling into a steady rhythm, or the clean, instant blue of the gas flame, were the everyday sounds of our kitchen. For newcomers to our home, their attention would inevitably be drawn to the silent stories etched onto our daily use vessels. A plate with a gentle inward curve or a vessel bearing the mark of a forceful dent were not simply imperfections. They conveyed tales of boundless boyhood games played outside and vessels were dented inside the house. Only we, the three musketeers of mischief, understood the stories behind those dents.

Our village, a comforting embrace of familiar faces and winding lanes, offered a brotherhood of friends. Yet, our playgrounds were limited and fiercely claimed, the single cricket ground where loyalties were drawn in the dust, the solitary volleyball court echoing with spirited shouts, the dusty kabaddi patch where grunts and breathless chants filled the air. Only the parched, cracked earth of the summer fields offered a truly untamed expanse for our adventures.

1986, Pants were our fashion statement

The essence of the village life was found in its unspoken network of care. We children were always under the gentle observation of village elders and well-wishers. The proverb, "It takes a village to raise a child," was not merely a saying but the foundation of our upbringing. Our parents, respected for their service to the community, frequently received updates about our daily activities, both achievements and mischief, shared with genuine concern. This informal network served as an early warning system, a human equivalent of social media, rapidly conveying information about our actions. Complaints, often delivered with affection, traveled swiftly. There seemed to be a certain satisfaction in sharing such stories, a cultural trait less common or understood in different parts of the world, where unsolicited feedback about children is often unwelcome.

We didn't actively seek out fights or arguments, but if they came our way, we certainly wouldn't step aside. We were not inherently troublesome children, but rather full of energy, our days filled with games and exploration. Our after school routine was consistent. We would come home wash away the day's dust, change into play clothes, and enjoy a brief period of freedom until the 6 p.m. curfew. These hours were governed by familiar parental instructions, "No fighting, no hitting anyone, no bad language, keep your clothes clean. Do not get hurt, and above all, do not fight with your brothers. If you do, I will not like it!" Such pronouncements, common in households worldwide, were not mere suggestions at the time, they carried the weight of unspoken consequences.

Family picture, probably one of many,
when we were young

Living in a village brought its own set of worries for our parents. They would bristle at any talk about their children, dread complaints, and lived with the constant fear of snakes. The place we lived had many types of snakes, some poisonous, and people even died from snakebites. Our bicycle rides brought their own share of anxiety, with the fear of unforeseen accidents lurking around every bend. We lived very close to the national highway, and though bicycles were allowed, we rode those roads as if they were any other street. But perhaps their deepest worry, the one that truly made their hearts pound, was water, especially open wells.

Sharath and Sudheer, both natural swimmers, took to water with remarkable ease. My own experience with swimming was nearly disastrous, marked by a struggle against the depths. During the intense summer heat, they would leave with friends around 10 a.m. and not return until the sun began to set. Sudheer, especially, was known for his swimming skills and often challenged others in the group. He was always the first to enter the water and the last to leave, his skin glistering in the sunlight. Occasionally, if Sharath wanted to return earlier, Sudheer's reluctance would lead to sibling fights. Absorbed in their wrestling, they would lose track of time and eventually return home close to the expected hour. Mom, with her keen ability to interpret our behaviour, could always detect when something was amiss. Initially unaware of their swimming activities, she became more apprehensive once she realised their abilities, making her hesitant to allow extended swimming sessions. We seemed to keep our parents in a constant state of vigilance. Balancing demanding work while raising three energetic children was undoubtedly challenging. We started learning about our parents' sacrifices, such as remaining in our small village and not pursuing higher positions. Yet many other unspoken choices were likely made to provide us with the freedom to grow within our community. They taught us the distinctions between good, bad, and unacceptable behaviour.

Not sure why Dad is missing

Our parents placed a high value on education. Mom, passionate about reading, pursued higher education for over four years while raising us. She believed that education brought status, prosperity, wisdom, and happiness. Their aspiration was for at least one of us to become a doctor, a profession they deeply respected, especially as Mom worked in the health department. She admired doctors for their role as lifesavers and their esteemed position in society. Although she hoped I would become a doctor, circumstances led me elsewhere. Had I become a doctor, I sometimes wonder if our parents might have lived longer. I chose engineering due to my grades and financial considerations. Sharath also became an engineer, while Sudheer pursued a degree in agriculture, following his own interests. Today, we all work in our chosen professions.

Sudheer continues his work in a seed research and production company, contributing to food production, and has never regretted his decision to become an agricultural scientist. Sharath began his career as an independent contractor, building houses, and later dedicated himself to providing quality education to those in need in small villages. Although there are no doctors in our immediate family, Mom once hoped for a daughter-in-law who would be a doctor. However, this aspiration did not materialise, nor have any of her grandchildren entered the medical profession.

Our parents upheld strict values and demonstrated disciplined, committed social conduct. They were religious, considerate, and always willing to help others. Dad, who had many friends, was widely respected for his character and behaviour. His experience in the defense forces instilled a high level of discipline, which he sought to impart to us. Although he never resorted to physical punishment, he commanded respect through his presence. Mom was gentle yet direct, often approaching matters with a clear yes or no. Reflecting on her career in government organisations, I am struck by how she maintained such decisiveness amid complexity. She was ambitious for us, expecting a high standard during our upbringing. Having faced many challenges, she recognised that survival required both care and discipline. At that time, parents believed it was easy for children to stray from the right path, so she emphasised on hard work, challenging status quo, and nurturing big dreams for our future. Education and moral character were equally important to her. She had limited support while we were growing up, aside from occasional visits to our grandparents during school holidays. Most of the time, we were her constant companions at home. Our parents understood that children learn by example, and they were careful in their interactions. We never witnessed them argue or raise their voices until we were in our teens. Many of their personal matters remained private until we were adults. In essence, they were teaching us how to live.

As a first generation working woman, first woman to work among siblings and known circles, Mom may not have anticipated the full demands of her responsibilities. Her days began well before dawn, waking up, preparing breakfast, packing lunch, and catching the early bus to reach her office in time, returning home exhausted after 6 p.m. This demanding routine persisted for many years. Although Dad provided support, the stress of this lifestyle affected her health. When we were especially mischievous, her frustration sometimes manifested in the dents on our kitchen vessels. In the face of these hardships, Mom remained our steady compass. She balanced her boundless love with a firm discipline, driven by a singular desire to see us grow into men of character. Though she lived under the relentless weight of constant pressure at a pace that likely paved the way for her hypertension, she never let us feel the strain. Our parents were remarkably generous, prioritising our growth above all else. Whether it was cricket gear, footballs, or bicycles, they ensured we had every tool we needed to dream and play.

When we all graduated and started working, the proud looks on our parents' faces whenever someone complimented their children, was a sight to behold. That feeling was deeply encouraging, and all the pain they had endured for so many years felt truly rewarding. This had come at the cost of listening to other parents' complaints, school messages, and community whispers. Once, at the age of seven, Sudheer ventured off with his friends to see distant caves and saints who lived several kilometres from home. The long hours stretched into late night, filling our parents and other villagers with fear and anxiety until his return. Sudheer's fascination with a double decker bus once led him to slip out of the house. When he saw the bus, he followed it without knowing how to find his way back home. We had nearly lost him, rescued only by divine grace, when Dad found him crying carried by a stranger to the police station. While learning to swim, I once almost drowned, pulled from the well's depths by our grandfather's quick action, his suspicion aroused by my sudden silence. These were moments that, though we might recount them casually now, must have been deeply painful for our parents. Once we grew up, they were probably very happy then.

We always fought as kids, and that continued even after we started working. We had our share of big arguments, but they never affected our relationships. But these never impacted our relationships. Like any growing adults, we were busy in our own worlds, trying to build our own careers and make a difference. Our parents were proud of their upbringing. Even today, we are recognised as the postmaster's or Jayakka's children. They have given us their name, identity, spirituality, love, and affection. Their legacy is too big to carry, being their children is truly a God's gift. While they disciplined us during our early days, they became friends after a certain period. They respected our views and thoughts, encouraged us to make our own decisions. We had the freedom and independence though they always watched over us. If a decision went wrong, they stood by us and said, "It's alright. Dust yourself off and keep moving. Be careful next time."

Many times in our own parenting, we look back and learn from our parents. While much has changed from then to now, the essence of parenting still remains the same.

Unfortunately, our children never saw their grandfather, but they were well cared for and had a great time with their grandmother. She knew how to take care of Ben and Alan and guided them in her wisdom. We often faced the brunt as we could not scold them in front of her.

2001, Just before Sharath and Sudheer's marriage

Today, we strive to keep our family culture alive, ensuring that our actions mirror the values we were taught. We aim to move through the world with the same integrity and grace, upholding the high standards of the legacy our parents so painstakingly built. Given the chance, we would choose to be part of the same parents again and again. We are not perfect, but we know how to accept our quirks and live to the next level. What we are today is a clear result of the sacrifice, love, affection, and discipline of our parents. The kindness and affection was a blessing from our parents, we are learning to attain their wisdom, and we will forever strive to be Jayamma & Daniel's children. The dents on the vessels were shaping us to be better people. Each dent was designing our future, teaching, and setting discipline in us.

Every mark on those stainless steel vessels recorded a Mom's exhaustion, a Dad's quiet disapproval, and the uncontainable energy of three brothers. The "Musketeers" were not merely playing, they were testing the boundaries of their world. When our Mom struck a vessel in frustration, she was not simply reacting to mischief, she was "hammering" her sons into better men.

The vessels lost their shape so that we could find ours. The comfort and career ambitions our parents surrendered became the 'soft metal' in our lives, an essential, yielding strength that enabled us to grow into men of character and purpose.

CHAPTER 3
HOME SWEET HOME

Even before I understood the word 'home', I understood movement. As with many government employees, my parents' lives were shaped by frequent transfers, typically every three to four years. I often reflect on how our story might have differed had they not chosen to return to Dad's ancestral village in 1973. Several significant factors influenced their decision to reconnect with our familial roots.

In 1970 we lived in Divanarapalya, Bangalore. Life followed a distinct rhythm, though it was often overshadowed by Mom's anxieties. Each cycle ride was an act of duty and risk. I recall stories of Dad cycling five kilometres to the HMT factory post office each day, navigating rough, unpaved roads. Mom, employed at the local hospital, bore the emotional burden of the accidents she witnessed, her concern for Dad heightened by the ever present risk posed by the HMT buses known for rash driving. I was a toddler then and my younger brother, Sharath was an infant. During those early years, the steady presence of Dad's mother provided comfort and stability as she cared for us while Mom fulfilled her professional duties.

Dad's profound desire to be close to his parents also influenced our move. After serving nine years in the Army and retiring early because of a persistent peptic ulcer that required surgery in Calcutta, he developed a heightened sense of filial responsibility and duty. As the only son, he felt compelled to support his ageing Dad, a small scale farmer who managed a few acres along with a couple of buffaloes and cows, their milk a daily staple. This longing for his roots exerted a strong influence, drawing us away from the rapidly expanding city of Bangalore.

Although Bangalore is often regarded as a city of opportunity, it paradoxically introduced instability into our lives. The city's favourable climate, numerous parks and lakes, and highly educated population attracted many, making it desirable for government employees. However, transfers were frequent and unpredictable, often disregarding the family's evolving needs. The prospect of Mom working in one part of the city and Dad in another corner, combined with inadequate public transportation and our inability to afford a private vehicle, signalled mounting difficulties. Consequently, relocating from Bangalore appeared to be the most rational path towards achieving stability.

Mom's uncle, a respected member in the health department, played a pivotal role in our relocation. Through his influence, for the first time, the chaos softened, Mom secured a transfer to Beechaganahalli, a quiet village near my grandparents. Her brother Jayamama, who worked as a school teacher in Beechanganhalli, and his wife Prema aunty who was also Mom's friend and worked at the local hospital, provided a supportive environment. The longstanding friendship between Jayamama and Dad, which began during Dad's family's tenancy in Mom's childhood home, later working together as teachers, further strengthened our familial ties. Although my recollections from that period are limited, I have been told that their support was invaluable during those years.

The Beechaganahalli house was modest, a linear arrangement of a verandah where the village life unfolded before us, a small living room that echoed with our laughter and occasional squabbles, a kitchen fragrant with simmering spices, and a tiny backyard. All perhaps twelve by twenty-five feet, yet it held our entire world. We didn't perceive its size as a limitation, it was simply "home" for us, and the small lane where people are more connected.

Picture of the house we lived in 50 years back and Sudheer was born here.

I have a vivid memory of the narrow passage between the living room and the kitchen, and the built-in cupboard that housed our cherished Murphy radio. That radio was our window to the world, its warm glow illuminating our evenings as Mom and Dad listened to the news and the melodious film songs (Mukesh and Md Rafi were his favourite singers, Dev Anand, Sunil Dutt and A Nageshwara Rao were his favourite actors). It was in this humble dwelling that our youngest brother, Sudheer, arrived. Dad, by then, was the Sub Postmaster in Gudibande, and his daily commute was a long route. Perhaps this is how my own commute to school began, as I was studying at a school thirty-five kilometres away from the village and making the journey every day at the age of seven. Later, I stayed with my maternal grandparents to attend a good school in Chikkaballapur. While living in this village, I witnessed firsthand a very rudimentary form of food delivery. Mom would meticulously pack a three tiered dabba (steel box), entrusting it to a bus driver in the morning and the empty containers returning on the afternoon bus. This was meticulously done for over three years, a silent act of community. It was quite common, especially in villages, when work took people far away and food outside was either unaffordable or unavailable. In our case, the driver, Chinappa, was Dad's cousin and had also served in the Army as a jeep driver. The drivers accepted occasional gifts as tokens of our gratitude and were often guests at village festivals or family functions.

Our move to Gudibande in 1977 marked a significant transition, as we suddenly found ourselves with more space in the post office quarters. Space arrived, but permanence did not. It was only the second time we had lived in a double storey house, evoking faint memories of earlier homes near railway lines in Bidadi and Anekal, where the sound of passing trains was ever present. In Gudibande, Mom appeared relieved to finally have multiple rooms, giving us boys and themselves their own space. Her transfer to the local hospital reunited her with close friends, Radhamani and Sumitramma, whose laughter filled Mom's routine and our new home. However, this sense of spaciousness was fleeting, as our next house, though equally large, felt more crowded and less open. It was here that Mom pursued senior professional training, perhaps drawing inspiration from the environment. Despite these changes, permanence remained elusive. Dad's profession required frequent relocations, akin to the itinerant communities in India, as our moves were dictated by government postings. Postmasters are expected to be available at all hours for urgent telegrams or calls, often lived in attached quarters. In Gudibande alone, we lived in four different houses, each move bringing its own challenges. Mom's promotion led to another relocation, this time to the hospital quarters, which contrasted sharply with the comfort we had begun to take for granted. The stability we sought by leaving Bangalore seemed increasingly unattainable. After seven years, we moved to Peresandra, hoping it would finally provide a sense of permanence. Public transport was limited, and in some villages was entirely absent, requiring Mom to walk many kilometres to serve the community. Demonstrating her resourcefulness and determination, Mom began learning to ride a scooter. That scooter changed Mom from dependent to indomitable, allowing her cover the long distances between villages and meet the demands of caring for three children.

Although the process was challenging and included moments that tested her confidence, she ultimately became a skilled rider. Over more than twenty years of riding, she had never been in an accident, a remarkable testament to her skill, commitment, and capability.

In front of Gudibande home - riding practice. Sharath as pillion rider and Vasantamma checking on her skills.

In Peresandra, Dad rekindled old friendships, having studied with many from the village, and enjoyed the camaraderie of a close-knit community where everyone knew one another. We settled in, finding a sense of belonging and a gentle rhythm to daily life. Mom soon came to be known as "Scooter Madam", becoming a familiar figure on the village roads, her scooter symbolising both independence and dedication. As her mobility increased, so did her responsibilities, and she devoted herself to serving the community. Our schooling continued, my brothers formed their own social circles, while I remained more reserved in the village as I didn't have many classmates in the village except for Krishna. However, our stability was again disrupted when Dad was unexpectedly transferred back to Gudibande. After nine moves since 1971, this felt particularly difficult. The repeated relocations, the constant disruptions, and the underlying anxiety became burdens we carried, often without fully understanding their impact. My own later experiences with frequent moves, ten times in twenty-five years, made me acutely aware of the challenges and personal toll of such instability. Even returning to familiar places did not feel like a homecoming, as time had altered both the environment and our perceptions. This was especially challenging for my parents, who were at the height of their careers and striving to provide stability for us during our formative years. Without a permanent home, moving every three years was difficult, particularly as we approached higher education, which required a more stable foundation. Gradually, the desire for a home of our own took root in Mom's heart, a significant aspiration for a middle class family seeking security and a permanent address. The values my parents instilled in us led us, their children, to prioritise home ownership early in our lives. Despite their government positions, our lifestyle was modest. Just as my parents began planning for a permanent home, fate intervened. Dad was posted back to Peresandra, but this time to a different post office. After enjoying the relative comfort of our previous homes with its spacious living room, two bedrooms, large kitchen, dining area, and backyard, we found ourselves in a much smaller space, just 12 by 20 feet for the five of us. The cramped conditions heightened tensions and frustrations. Finding rental housing in villages was challenging, as most homes were built for personal use rather than investment. Fortunately, we soon found relief by moving into the upstairs portion of Mom's best friend's home, where the increased space and natural light provided much needed comfort.

Peresanda home that was part of our lives, this where our lives were defined and built deep relationships,

There were three rooms, larger this time, with a wide verandah where we often congregated, the open space a balm to our cramped spirits. By now, the tally of moves stood at eleven, and our own quiet longing for a permanent anchor for our family intensified. Then a sliver of hope appeared, as a plot of land became available, with a friend of Dad's offering it at a price that seemed almost too good to be true. The dream of ownership, so long deferred, flickered to life. Mom and Dad, with a shared determination, marshalled their resources. Mom parted with her precious gold, each piece a silent sacrifice, and secured a loan from her office. Dad followed suit. They even reached out to family and friends for small loans, pooling every rupee to secure that 1600 square foot plot in Chikkaballapur. It was a dream, years in the making, as the very act of owning land marked a significant milestone in our cultural context. Maybe we didn't understand the feeling until we ourselves purchased land in our own names. We had the land, a tangible piece of our future, but the daunting task of building a home still loomed large. Yet, we had taken that crucial first step. For Mom, the purchase held a particular resonance, the land lay directly opposite her childhood home, a poignant connection to her past. Even Dad remembered the area from his early years when his family had rented there. But as the Kannada saying goes, "Manina runa and annada runa devaru baridirabeku", "mannina runa" (ಮಣ್ಣಿನ ಋಣ) and "annada runa" (ಅನ್ನದ ಋಣ), refer to the debt owed to the land and the food it provides. It is a powerful cultural expression that emphasises gratitude, belonging, and duty towards one's homeland and the sustenance it provides. We didn't yet know the twists and turns our destiny held.

Mom's friend Savithramma was developing a new layout in Peresandra, and Mom, ever pragmatic, considered purchasing a smaller plot there. Peresandra was close to my grandparents, who owned five acres of land nearby, offering a potential retirement haven and a way to remain connected to family. Additionally, my parents had cultivated strong relationships within the community in Peresandra and maintained proximity to our farmland. Meanwhile, the issue of Dad not residing in the designated post office quarters became an issue. Those quarters were dark, poorly ventilated, and oppressive, making the prospect of returning unappealing after experiencing greater comfort elsewhere. However, a disagreement between Mom and her friend led us back to the very quarters we had hoped to avoid. The cramped, airless rooms seemed to reflect the underlying tension. Amidst this uncertainty, we began constructing our own house in Peresandra. The emotional significance of building a home was profound, especially given the societal challenges and feelings of helplessness my parents faced at the height of their careers. The promise of a permanent residence stood in stark contrast to years of transient living, with memories of leaky roofs and damp walls serving as constant reminders of our past. My cousin Kiran Victor, an engineer, contributed his expertise to the design, and relatives offered their support to help realise Mom's vision. Although the plans were impressive, the financial burden was considerable, with each construction expense straining our resources. A loan from LIC Housing Finance provided some assistance, but it was insufficient. Once again, Mom's gold, her streedhanam, traditionally accumulated for such emergencies became our financial lifeline. Persistent challenges at home and mounting financial pressures continued to test our resilience.

We were compelled to stay a while longer in the Peresandra post office quarters, as construction was paused after we had exhausted all conventional financial options, including family loans, friendly advances, and formal housing loan financing. The necessity of selling the Chikkaballapur plot, our initial symbol of hope, located directly across from Mom's childhood home, was a devastating setback. Hope, once bought, was sold back to survival, though as children we did not fully grasp the extent of our parents' disappointment. High interest rates on informal loans further eroded their peace of mind, leading to tension at home. Dad, always stoic, had long harboured concerns about the scale and cost of the house. The atmosphere at home was often tense with unspoken worries. At this stage, my siblings and I were navigating adolescence and the demands of professional studies. Having completed my degree, I chose to remain at home, providing silent support to Mom as she worked tirelessly to complete our house. The process of building our home over one and a half years was marked by a range of emotions, joy, sadness, tears, and constant challenges. My parents were unprepared for the complexities involved in engaging relatives as engineers, bricklayers, carpenters, and electricians. While it had its advantages, it also introduced additional challenges.

Home Sweet Home

Finally, the auspicious housewarming of our "God's Grace, Daniel's Cottage" on Friday, August 7, 1993, coincided with Varalakshmi Vratam, the festival of wealth and prosperity. What a long and arduous journey it had been for our family. We had started with so little, enduring thirteen moves in twenty years, weathering the indignity of substandard living conditions and the sting of social condescension, navigating internal challenges, selling Mom's cherished possessions, and living frugally for years to clear the mounting debt. Yet, amidst all this turmoil, my parents remained steadfast in their commitment to our education. Their eldest and second sons became engineers, and the third an agricultural research graduate, a testament to their unwavering belief in the transformative power of learning.

Donning the home

I can still vividly recall the raw emotion etched on their faces that day, with tears that mingled joy, pain, and sheer exhaustion.

Dad, who had never envisioned such a grand house, perhaps found the purest joy in its completion, his simpler needs overshadowed by the profound satisfaction of seeing Mom's dream realised. He had lived her dream, a quiet pillar of support through every twist and turn. Differences, as they inevitably do, had surfaced, but his unwavering support never faltered. My parents, in their late forties, finally stood on the threshold of a dream realised through sheer grit and unwavering determination. They had worked for it, they had sacrificed for it, and in doing so, they etched a powerful lesson in our young hearts about the unwavering pursuit of one's aspirations. Like Abdul Kalam so eloquently stated, "A dream is not something that you see while sleeping, it is something that does not let you sleep." My parents had lived that truth. It was our privilege to witness Mom's indomitable spirit, her refusal to yield, drawing strength from every flicker of hope to manifest a dream born from the crucible of hardship, humiliation, and a deep seated sense of helplessness.

In that house, built with their sweat and tears, both my parents finally found a measure of peace. They transformed bricks, cement, and mortar into a sanctuary of love and tranquillity, a place of rest and rejuvenation, a space where our family bonds deepened, and a symbol of our hard-earned identity and shared joy. Mom constantly wanted our friends and family to visit and stay with us in our new home.

Although our parents faced significant challenges in acquiring their first home, their blessings and guidance enabled us, their children, to experience greater abundance. I often joked with Mom that she eventually became the proud owner of seven homes. From 1993 onward, she never lived in a rental property until her passing in 2017. It was likely their wish that we would not endure the same struggles or humiliation they had faced. Parents strive to provide the best for their children and to ensure their success in life.

The profound truth here is that a house is built with bricks, but a home is built with determination and love. Our parents didn't just build a cottage, they built a fortress against the "humiliation of the rental" and the "sting of social condescension." When they finally opened the doors to *Daniel's Cottage* in 1993, the tears on their faces weren't just for the new walls, they were for the end of a long, weary journey. They traded their gold and their youth so that their sons would never have to understand the word "transient."

CHAPTER 4
VISIONARY AND DETERMINED SISTER

Life's Vision - Vasanthamma (Sister)

This is the story of a person who demonstrated extraordinary grit, unwavering grace, and a clear vision that guided her through a life lived on her own terms. To truly understand her, it is essential to understand the world she was born into.

I invite you to reflect on a time that feels both distant and immediate. Our family was not affluent.

Our Parents humble beginnings

We were nine siblings, all living together in the CSI Hospital quarters in Chikkaballapur, near the church. Our lives were closely connected to the missionary doctors who resided and worked there. These doctors, who had come from England with a genuine desire to serve the poor, became integral to our family's story. We held them in high regard, and their guidance shaped many aspects of our upbringing. Their influence endures, even in 2025, heirloom furniture, dinner sets, and flower pots still grace our homes, serving as tangible reminders of that era. The doctors played a significant role in guiding our brothers towards vocational training.

Mom during her teens!

Between 1962 and 1970 in South India, ordinary families often experienced conformity, scarcity, and low literacy. Opportunities were limited, and life paths were typically determined by others. While the doctors' encouragement provided our brothers with paths to financial independence, societal expectations of the time meant that our eldest sister stayed back to support the household and help her brothers pursue their training. One became a carpenter, another a teacher, and another a driver, each building a life of dignity and self-reliance. Her contribution followed a quieter path. She set aside the opportunity for further formal education, choosing instead to support Mom and care for the younger siblings, becoming the steady foundation on which much of our family's progress rested.

1984 Gudibande home with two of our brothers

When it was Jayakka's turn, the expectation was that she would pursue nursing training. However, at just fourteen years old, she boldly challenged this path. With remarkable determination, she stated, "I don't want to go to nursing training, I want to study, I will finish my SSLC (10th Grade) and then think about training." This decision represented an extraordinary act of courage, as she asserted her right to education during a period characterised by conformity.

ANM training batch

She shared a close bond with our brother Jayanna, who offered her unwavering support. The younger siblings Samuel, Prabhakar, Sudarshan, and I did not experience the same direct influence from the doctors, as they had left the country by the time we reached school age. Consequently, we relied on Jayakka for support and guidance. She became our informal leader and caretaker, especially when our parents went to the late night movies. She would tell us stories to ensure we felt safe and calm. During the day, she led our play, engaging in activities such as running, climbing trees, and cycling with remarkable energy. She was attentive to our youngest brother's safety, often securing him to her back with a veil. Her enthusiasm for cycling enabled her to ride a scooter later in her career, which was a pioneering achievement for a woman in our district. Additionally, she possessed a sensitive and artistic nature, spending hours drawing and painting landscapes. This artistic inclination has continued in her youngest son, Sudheer.

*With her Jayanna, Akka, my Cousin Viji
and Nephew Kiran*

From a young age, she developed a passion for reading, frequently borrowing library books. She was proficient in reading both Telugu and Kannada. At fourteen, she translated a Telugu novel into Kannada, demonstrating her concentration and unique abilities. She was fluent in four languages and, after learning English, could communicate in five, Kannada, Telugu, Tamil, Malayalam and English. Her intellectual independence was a defining trait, rooted in a strong and assertive personality inherited from Mom, Rajamma, who communicated with clarity despite her reserved nature. Jayakka was direct yet considerate, critical without cynicism, and always refrained from speaking ill of others. However, the pressures associated with her genuine character contributed to health challenges later in life, including high blood pressure and diabetes.

Her most definitive act of grit came when she was twenty-one and chose to marry our brother's friend, Daniel.

*Bava and akka marriage picture in front of
our family home 1969,*

During this period, societal expectations for women were shaped by family honor and caste. Choosing a love marriage was considered rebellious and carried significant social stigma, particularly for lower middle class families. This act of defiance risked social exclusion and loss of family support. Despite these challenges, she maintained a clear vision for her life and her chosen partner. Jayanna supported her again as he did earlier when he took her to Bangalore and joined her for ANM training against the will of the family elders. She had to take the brunt of her other brothers for a while after finishing the course.

1969 taken at studio

Following her marriage, she dedicated herself to rural communities, often traveling between distant villages on foot to provide essential health services. Dad supported her by caring for her first child, Deepak, while Bava served in the military. Upon Bava's (brother-in-law) retirement from military and subsequent employment with the Indian Postal Service at the HMT factory in Bangalore, my sister, Bava, and Deepak relocated to Divanarapalya. Within 1.5 years of her first job as ANM, she challenged the status quo and applied for training to become HV, a health visitor. Her selection for the training was also the reason to move to Bangalore along with Bava's new job. During this period, my sister trained at KC General Hospital in Bangalore, facing numerous challenges.

One of her greatest challenges was working against the traditional expectations of her in-laws' agricultural family. Having a working daughter-in-law who was also a government employee was unprecedented and a source of pride, yet it also brought social pressure due to her absence from home. My sister managed these expectations with remarkable composure, maintaining her professional responsibilities while supporting her family and guiding her siblings. Her example was so influential that Bava's eldest sister, who had only completed eighth grade, later pursued nurse training and became an Auxiliary Nurse Midwife.

Her clear vision for her children's future was a driving force. She and Bava wanted them to get the best education, considering schools like the Sainik School or St. Joseph's School at Bangalore. That was the very reason they moved to Bangalore, for a better lifestyle, education, and schools. Also, they had seen that Bangalore was giving them more opportunities. Sharath, their second son, was born in Bangalore and life there was becoming challenging. However, they had to move back to Beechaganahalli as Bava needed to care for his aging parents. Additionally, his daily cycling route to work at HMT factory had become increasingly hazardous. In this village, where Jayanna, my second brother, was a teacher and our sister-in-law worked as an ANM, a beautiful reunion of friends and siblings took place. It was here that my sister welcomed a third son, Sudheer.

Throughout her life, Jayakka was a person who never gave up, she was determined and committed. She was the engine of our family, capable of pulling us through hard times and pushing us toward our goals. She didn't sign up for conformity but handled every challenge with grace. A master of balancing her work and family, she did so even at the expense of her own health. Her work was her worship. Born a middle child, she was undeniably the centre of our attention.

All the family members

For 63 years, her presence was a constant in my life. Our experiences together encompassed love, affection, misunderstandings, and laughter. Her absence has left a significant void and a deep sense of loneliness. Yet, in our grief, we recognise the many lives she influenced and how her resilience, grace, and determination continue to inspire us. Her story encourages us to pursue purposeful lives guided by our own vision.

Whether consciously or not, our lives remained interwoven through every phase, and the pictures below confirm the truth of our bond throughout life.

The profound truth here is that grace is not the absence of struggle but the composure one maintains while breaking barriers. Jayakka chose a love marriage despite the social stigma, walked kilometers on foot to serve rural patients, and balanced the heavy traditional expectations of her in-laws with the demands of a government career. She traded her own comfort and health to ensure her siblings and children never had to settle for a life "determined by others."

Her vision was her compass, and her grit was her fuel. Jayakka was the "engine" of the family. She wasn't just living her life, she was engineering a future for everyone around her. Whether she was tying her youngest brother to her back with a veil to keep him safe, translating novels between languages, or becoming the first woman in the district to master a scooter, she was constantly expanding the boundaries of what was possible.

CHAPTER 5
LIFE HAPPENS

The arrival of February in India marks a gentle turning of the seasons, as winter loosens its grip and the first whispers of warmth begin to stir. It's a time when the winds pick up, a natural invitation for us to head outdoors and showcase our kite flying prowess. Each of us brothers had our own way of crafting these colourful messengers and preparing their trailing lines. We'd meticulously add vibrant frills along the edges, giving them a festive flourish. The thread, our vital link to the skybound creations, was carefully strengthened to endure the tugs and pulls of the wind and the inevitable aerial contests.

During this season, the sky above our village was often crowded with kites, each symbolising the ambitions of its flyer. My brothers and I engaged in friendly competition, challenging one another as our voices and laughter resonated across the fields, often joined by friends. This competitive spirit extended beyond kite flying to activities such as top spinning, bicycle races, volleyball, marbles, matchbox cards, gilli-danda (tip cat), lagori, hide and seek, football, running with a tyre, and especially cricket, all approached with equal enthusiasm and intensity.

Our competitive spirit was most intense during cricket matches among ourselves. The playful yet sharp banter, often peaked during these games. Occasionally, the intensity led to actual disputes on the dusty pitch. In these moments, family bonds were temporarily set aside as each of us remained loyal to our respective teams. Similarly, during kite flying, we maintained a respectful distance, with the rooftops serving as our personal arenas. When a kite performed exceptionally well, we would sometimes secure its line to a sturdy fixture and leave for lunch or a snack, confident in its continued flight.

Even on the most favorable days, when a kite soared with ease, unexpected challenges could occur. Some kites would veer off course due to loss of control, while others would slowly descend. These moments underscored their inherent fragility. Despite our careful construction and handling, a kite could become unusable in an instant due to torn paper, broken tail, damaged frill, or snapped line. After such incidents, it no longer functioned as a true kite.

We gradually came to understand that life mirrors this unpredictability. Extended periods of uninterrupted happiness are uncommon, rather, life consists of intervals of comfort interrupted by unexpected challenges. These disruptions remind us of life's fragility and the necessity of preparedness.

A major disruption occurred when Dad, then only forty years old, suddenly collapsed at work at a time when Mom was away for supervisor training. Anand, a recently appointed colleague of Dad's, acted promptly and rushed Dad to the local hospital, after which he was transferred to a larger facility in Bangalore. Anand's actions were particularly inspiring, given his own recent bereavement and his new position through compassionate appointment. While he could not alter the final outcome of Dad's health, his intervention shielded our family from a potentially more difficult future. Losing Dad at such a young age would have significantly impacted Mom's aspirations, our education, and the dream of a family home.

We were fortunate that day, as Dad survived a severe heart attack. Despite his lean physique, abstinence from alcohol, low blood pressure, and military background, he was unexpectedly vulnerable. He did, however, frequently smoke beedis and drink tea. Nevertheless, he embodied discipline, loyalty, and dedication to his work. His professional ethics were exemplary, and he was highly skilled. His guiding principle, displayed on his desk, stated, "If you don't have anything to do, don't do it here." This message succinctly discouraged unproductive behaviour in public service.

Ready to go to Church

Following this health scare, Dad made notable changes to his lifestyle, reducing both tea consumption and smoking. His inherent discipline meant few other adjustments were necessary. For Mom, the event was deeply distressing. During Dad's heart attack, she was several hundred kilometers away, engaged in a year-long training program. She visited us monthly during breaks or emergencies, and we eagerly anticipated her return, especially for her cooking and the sweets she brought. In her absence, our grandmother from Halle Peresandra cared for us, displaying a leniency that we, as grandchildren, often took advantage of.

Dad recovered rapidly and resumed work within a month, though in a less demanding role. His colleagues, especially Anand, offered substantial support, often assuming extra responsibilities to aid Dad's recovery. Mom displayed remarkable resilience, never voicing complaints about her increased workload. Instead, she became more vigilant regarding Dad's medication and health. Our later experiences living abroad deepened our appreciation for life, a perspective less evident during our youth, when abundance sometimes dulled our awareness of its fragility.

Nearly forty years later, a similar crisis affected my brother Sudheer, who, at about the same age as Dad, suffered a major cardiac arrest. This was particularly shocking given his healthy lifestyle, he did not drink or smoke, maintained a healthy weight, worked diligently, and balanced his personal and professional life. One day after returning home from work, he went to sleep and was later found sweating profusely and struggling to breathe. Having recently relocated from Bangalore to Hyderabad with Sheeba, he was living independently from the rest of the family. Prabhakar Uncle, Sudheer's father-in-law, who was visiting, recognised the urgency, immediately took Sudheer to the hospital. Prabhakar uncle was a heart attack survivor, and seemed to be present there by providence. Doctors confirmed a significant heart attack, but Sudheer received timely treatment. The presence of both uncle and Anand at critical moments felt like a profound blessing for our family.

The news was deeply distressing for Mom. Sheeba demonstrated remarkable mental, physical, and spiritual strength, navigating the crisis with resilience and emerging even stronger. Sudheer, understandably, grappled with questions of fairness and meaning. Our experiences reinforced that life's unpredictability is ever present, while it is easy to acknowledge, enduring it is far more challenging. Just as a soaring kite can suddenly falter, so too can life's stability be disrupted, highlighting its fragility and our limited control.

This same unpredictability affected us on a bright day, May 2, 2002. Nearly a decade earlier, by 1993, my parents had achieved much of what they had aspired to. Their family home was completed, I had graduated as an engineer, Sharath was in his second year of Civil Engineering, and Sudheer had secured his seat in BSc Agriculture. Life seemed to be moving steadily forward, with my brothers pursuing professional courses and me beginning my career. My parents began searching for a suitable match when I was twenty-six, but initial efforts were unsuccessful. They favored an arranged marriage, which prioritises family compatibility, values, and stability over individual romance. Although my parents were open-minded in many ways, they maintained traditional views on marriage. I also realised I had not given the matter enough attention, nor considered its impact on my younger brothers. After career changes and starting a business which delayed the process, the tide finally turned when I met Asha, and she agreed to marry me, and we wed on June 22, 2000. The following year, on December 28, Sharath and Sudheer married Smitha and Sheeba.

2001 Last family picture of all of us together

The weddings were major occasions, attended by thousands of well-wishers. However, Dad fell ill before the ceremonies and required hospitalisation, making this period especially difficult for our family. Mom faced significant pressure, balancing Dad's care, wedding arrangements, and her professional duties. In retrospect, I realise I never asked her how she managed the physical, emotional, and financial challenges. Although we had attained some financial stability, the demands on Mom's mental health were substantial. This experience has since motivated me to regularly check on family and friends, understanding that simply listening can offer comfort and build trust.

On May 2, 2002, during the peak of summer, Dad was working in Bagepalli. He had recently transferred there from his demanding position at the Chikkaballapur head office, seeking a less stressful environment with fewer responsibilities. That afternoon, after stepping out of the shade, he experienced sudden dizziness and blurred vision. Believing it was due to something he had eaten, he dismissed the episode. However, after returning home and sleeping that night, he never fully regained his previous state of health.

The following morning, Mom noticed Dad's face was frozen in an unnatural stillness and his head held with an unusual rigidity. Realising the severity, she rushed him to RL Jalappa Hospital. The doctors conducted a thorough examination, our cousin Anand and his wife, Latha, who worked there, facilitated access to specialists. Ultimately, they determined that Dad had suffered a massive stroke, resulting in the loss of movement and speech. He survived but was left bedridden, unable to speak, feed himself, walk, or sit up without assistance.

This event caused deep grief and confusion within our family, prompting questions about fairness and destiny. The resulting helplessness echoed earlier hardships. Human vulnerability and the randomness of such events became unmistakably clear. Despite our attempts with alternative treatments, Dad's condition remained unchanged. The ongoing search for solutions became a constant and exhausting part of our daily lives.

Mom shouldered the primary caregiving role, bolstered by the constant support of Sharath, Sudheer, Smitha, and Sheeba. I had moved to Bangalore in 2001, leaving my business that I started in 1999. Although the business was successful, unclear roles among the three partners prompted me to leave before conflicts could arise. Despite the strain of Dad's illness, we believed we were navigating life with resilience and purpose. However, life's unpredictability soon exposed our vulnerability, fundamentally changing our circumstances and making it challenging to regain our previous sense of normalcy.

In the early hours of November 22, 2002, I received a call from Prabhakar uncle informing me of Dad's passing. He was on his way to pick us up enroute to Peresandra. The news brought a complex mix of emotional relief that

Dad was no longer confined to a non-responsive body, yet sorrow at his absence and the realisation that he would not witness our future achievements. There was also concern for Mom whether she would find relief from her caregiving responsibilities or face the deep grief of losing her partner of more than three decades.

Dad, while in the army

Everything changed rapidly. Dad was gone, and we would no longer see his gentle smile, his disciplined demeanour, the familiar weekend discussions about meals, or his quiet retreat for a pre-lunch whiskey. We had lost our straightforward military man, who cherished simplicity above all. We missed his presence in our lives. Even now, when confronted with important decisions, we often ask ourselves, "How would Dad have handled this?" and strive to follow that internal guidance.

We discovered that turbulence often leaves lasting effects, seldom resolving quickly or without consequences. This pattern recurred in our lives since 1983, with major events frequently disrupting periods of calm. In 1987, Mom underwent major surgery and was unable to work for over three months, spending extended periods in the hospital and with family in Tumkur. In 1988, Dad experienced a second, less severe heart attack and recovered. We also endured the loss of our grandfather, Dad's father, and several other relatives and friends in rapid succession. In 1995, a serious car accident involving Sudarshan Uncle, Rani Akka, and Sharath caused lasting injuries, though all survived. While it is easy to focus on these hardships, we learned to recognise when the worst had passed, express gratitude, and continue living with intention.

Humans naturally seek patterns and meaning as they navigate life. For several years, our family experienced relative stability. The births of Ben in 2004 and Alan in 2007 brought renewed joy, and we adapted to the evolving dynamics within our home and the broader world.

On October 18, 2007, our period of calm was abruptly interrupted when Mom became acutely unwell, her speech suddenly slurred and incomprehensible. We immediately took her to the hospital. Although I cannot conclusively blame the initial doctors, I continue to feel that Mom's care may not have been as comprehensive as necessary.

I remain convinced that her condition was not treated with adequate urgency, and that earlier intervention might have reduced the stroke's severity. Consequently, Mom was left with persistent stiffness in her right hand and leg. The situation was particularly poignant, as she had retired only eighteen months earlier after a forty-year medical career, serving numerous communities and assisting in hundreds of births, only to be let down by the very healthcare system she had supported.

We found ourselves reflecting on the situation of a woman who devoted her life to the well-being of others, retiring with the hope of enjoying time with family, friends, and her interests in agriculture and nature. Why did such misfortune befall her? As Les Brown aptly stated, "Life happens."

Moms retirement on 28th Feb 2006. A common scene in our family is that many of us go to the office when someone is getting retired, and silently tell them we are at home to support them

Mom demonstrated remarkable inner strength and determination. She did not give in to adversity, instead embracing physiotherapy and exercises to adapt to her new circumstances. Despite the limitations in her right leg and hand, she traveled to Jerusalem and Auckland, managing effectively. Adaptation became central to her life as she continually adjusted to new challenges. She faced difficulties directly, seldom complaining or indulging in self-pity. While moments of frustration were natural, she maintained her independence and consistently avoided burdening her family.

My interactions with Mom were consistently positive and encouraging. Even when faced with disrespect, she responded without bitterness. Although she was outspoken in her youth, she developed a gentle and polite manner over time. Despite significant losses and challenges including Dad's death, Sudheer's health issues, my distance from home, and limited contact with her grandchildren, she found ways to accept and make sense of these hardships, drawing comfort from her belief in a higher purpose. Her spirituality was personal rather than traditional, and she avoided contentious discussions. One of her lasting lessons was, "Let's agree to disagree and move on." She embodied many of Dad's philosophies, and we, her children, strive to uphold the values imparted by our parents.

Just as a kite that faces obstacles never fully regains its original freedom, our family underwent a comparable transformation. Life's unpredictability became a defining theme. This may be a universal truth that confronting challenges with adaptability and the right mindset can ease the journey. It is akin to moving with the current rather than resisting it.

We recognise that life unfolds unpredictably, requiring continual adaptation, the ability to let go, and the discipline to establish sustaining routines. Beyond mere survival, we have learned that a meaningful life is often embodied by those who find joy in small moments. We now strive to live in that spirit, offering comfort, extending assistance, and choosing to go the extra mile whenever possible. Life has been generous to us, prompting us to consider how we can give back. In this journey of service and gratitude, we are guided by the enduring grace that characterised Mom's life.

CHAPTER 6
WOVEN LIVES, LASTING IMPRESSIONS

In an era marked by global connectivity and fragmented relationships, social media has become a crucial tool for rekindling connections with individuals who might otherwise fade from our lives. Unlike those who remain in their hometowns, we traverse a broad, interconnected world where finding common ground can be challenging. Nevertheless, platforms such as WhatsApp and Facebook serve as digital gathering places, enabling schoolmates to reunite after decades apart. Observing these reunions, I am reminded of a universal desire, to revisit cherished memories, to foster happiness, and to experience the warmth of extended family. While digital tools connect us our family roots were nourished by physical journeys. Historically, families undertook long pilgrimages, often combining spiritual journeys with exploration. For those preoccupied with daily responsibilities, these pilgrimages offered a rare opportunity to step away from routine and be fully present, focusing on spirituality and nature. We were fortunate to experience these moments without the distractions of modern technology. During these gatherings with extended family, deep bonds and mutual reliance developed, often without our conscious awareness. Our family, like many others, participated in this tradition. These journeys were not solely about reaching a destination, they centered on shared laughter, storytelling, and the creation of enduring memories.

I often wondered how certain family members remained so keen to travel every year or two. I found myself questioning how they possessed such an abundance of time and resources, yet I never dared to ask. Over the years, the frequency of these travels has waned as life shifted, priorities evolved, and our needs changed. Yet Sudarshan Uncle still carries that same zeal and continues to plan journeys for his Church or Rotary community, always extending an invitation for the family to join.

These trips and the memories they birthed remain with us forever. Mom was always keen to go. At times, she could prioritise the journey, while at other times, life's demands took precedence. Thanks to her spirit and these family trips, we were blessed to travel across most of South India. It is a true blessing to have such people in our lives and to share such deep rooted bonds within a family.

Mom's Singapore visit - Universal Studio Sentosa

The rhythm of shared life, from daily dinners to weekend adventures, truly formed the bedrock of our existence, fostering connection and creating memories that shaped us. Shared family experiences are the fertile ground where memories blossom, and emotional well-being takes root.

These range from the mundane comfort of family meals to the grand adventures of vacations. On weekdays, even from a young age, it hummed with the busy rhythm of a nuclear, working parent household. Mornings were a whirlwind with the kids scrambling for school, Mom preparing for work, and lunch being packed all at once. A leisurely breakfast together was a rare luxury, but the dinner table became our sacred space. No matter the stage of life whether we were growing up, navigating adulthood, or raising our own children, dinner remained a steadfast family ritual. Unknowingly, we honed this practice for years, a vital anchor in an increasingly disconnected world, especially as mobile phones began to claim the attention of our growing children.

With Koreans church group

Weekends, especially Sundays, stood apart as our only respite after six days of work. Our Sunday routine was memorable, a relaxed breakfast, followed by household cleaning, washing bicycles and scooters, and completing chores before lunch. Afternoons were reserved for ironing clothes, a task Dad approached with military precision. He insisted on perfectly pressed garments, reflecting his disciplined standards. No one was permitted to leave the house in wrinkled attire, a rule deeply ingrained in our daily lives. The day also included rest, walks, indoor games, or cricket and volleyball. Evenings concluded with dinner and the ritual of polishing shoes for the week ahead. Dad believed that shoes should be polished to a mirror-like shine, a standard I struggled to achieve. This was our life before television became part of our lives. Our entertainment often centered on touring talkies, which were temporary cinemas set up in rural areas after harvest season. These makeshift theaters, housed in large tents, brought communities together under the stars. We would sit on the sand, surrounded by hundreds, captivated by the film. These experiences, shared with family and friends, created lasting memories and contributed to the rich tapestry of our early years.

The essence of growing up in small villages was found in the communal celebration of festivals, which extended far beyond individual family gatherings. The villagers, though relaxed in demeanor, demonstrated a remarkable approach to life and happiness. These festivals were collective events, enlivened by overnight storytelling such as Harikathe, a composite art form combining narrative, mime, and music focused on devotional themes, and Burra Katha, a rhythmic oral tradition presenting social and mythological dramas. I vividly remember Channapa Reddy, a respected teacher and family friend, whose commanding presence brought numerous social and historical plays to life and captivated audiences. While national festivals were important, it was the local village celebrations, harvest festivals, temple centric events, folk entertainment, storytelling, acrobatics, puppetry, and traditional games that left the most profound impression. Growing up in this multicultural environment was a continuous celebration, enriching our senses and experiences.

Picture taken in our fields

Although our family was the only Christian household in the village, we never felt isolated. We received numerous invitations to feasts, often having to choose between several on the same day, and there was never any resentment. In return, we welcomed our neighbours during Christmas and other important occasions, fostering relationships that transcended religious differences. Even now, Sharath and Sudheer continue these traditions by returning to our ancestral village, ensuring our family's ties with people endures. The saying, "It takes a village to raise a child," aptly describes the extensive community support that shaped not only our upbringing but also our family's wellbeing. This network extended beyond immediate family, encompassing many individuals who played significant roles in our development. The community spirit, characterised by shared joy and mutual support, was instrumental in creating lasting memories and a deep sense of belonging. Many from our village

, as well as our parents' friends including Chinnapiah, Geriga Reddy, Channapa Reddy, SVR, LN Reddy, Anand Murthy, BMR, Keshava Reddy, Bhoopal Reddy, Raghunath Reddy, Jayaram, Jeenaraju, Ashwath Reddy, and Dinaapally Nagaraju, greatly influenced our upbringing.

As we grew within the embrace of our community and friends, another defining avenue shaped who we were, our extended family. Mom's side alone boasted nine siblings, their children (our cousins) and even some grandchildren became our informal teachers during our family reunions, countless family gatherings, and church events. As a closely knit extended family, we had a cherished practice of travelling together for a week or two, exploring various places around Karnataka, a mix of pilgrimages and sightseeing. These trips were far more than mere excursions, they were a form of spiritual nourishment, deepening our faith and our understanding of a higher kindness and greatness. For us, it was never about rigid religion or the performance of ritual, it was about seeking a genuine, soulful connection.

Within that sacred space, a profound bonding took place among cousins, uncles, and aunts. In those days, we knew each other's hearts, we were a family so tightly woven that even the most distant relatives felt like immediate kin. Today, that closeness feels like a relic of a different era, as we find ourselves scattered across the world. There is a specific, heavy burden in trying to hold three to five generations together, a quiet pain that the elders of our family carry daily, a weight my own Mom bore as she watched the drapes of our togetherness begin to fray.

Picture with most of cousins of the family

Naturally, with three to four generations travelling together, differences arose. But through these journeys, we learned to live with those differences, to accept people just as they were. A striking memory is how our parents, particularly Mom, maintained a delicate balance. Mom, though she trusted others implicitly, found it hard to see her children corrected in front of her. This unspoken expectation, this feeling of having "failed" if we were corrected publicly, was a unique challenge within our closely knit family. Contrast this with the world we inhabit today, parents now often resist or even outright reject anyone from the community, friends, or even extended family correcting their children. This has led to a defensive culture, where one might hear the sentiment "Who the hell is he to tell us how to live?" far too often, and as a result, children miss out on the benefits of community living and the opportunity to develop mental toughness.

Society has transitioned from communal living to nuclear families, often accompanied by a belief in the superiority of modern knowledge. The concept that "it takes a village to raise a child" has diminished in urban environments and even in evolving villages, as technologies such as television and mobile phones have transformed the nature of human connection. These developments underscore a significant departure from the collective experiences that once naturally fostered lasting memories and intergenerational bonds, resulting in fragmented relationships and severe mental health issues.

While community living, extended families and friends taught us the art of harmonious coexistence, travel and reading were powerful complements, enriching our experiences and expanding our perspectives. We had incredible opportunities to travel as a family to tourist attractions, pilgrimages, and even across state borders. Short trips to Bangalore and Nandi Hills were backyard excursions, requiring no grand plans. But anything beyond those familiar places meant a significant discussion, sometimes even a minor family "fights," and elaborate planning. Beyond the many extended family adventures with cousins, aunts, and uncles, our family, just the 5 of us, embarked on a select few but deeply significant journeys to Mysore, Goa, and Velankanni.

One of such trips

Dad, privileged with Leave Travel Allowance (LTA) every two years, utilised it only three times. The trip to Velankanni, for instance, came many years later, although I personally visited Velankanni countless times with my cousins, Asha, Mom, and as part of larger extended family trips.

Goa trip

After returning from the army, Dad rarely spoke of God or his spiritual journey, yet he never once discouraged us from being spiritual. The one journey he made with us to Velankanni, however, remains etched in my memory as incredibly scary and nerve wracking. This was after our home was built and all of us had graduated. We planned a week-long LTA trip to Velankanni, travelling by train from Bangalore to Trichy, and then taking a local bus. After a few days there, as we began our return, we had dinner in Trichy before boarding the train back to Bangalore. In the dead of night, as the train cut through darkness and silence, a sudden commotion woke us. Mom was deeply worried. Dad was battling relentless diarrhoea, and despite Mom's usual emergency medical kit, there were no tablets to control it. He rapidly became dehydrated. Then, a sudden inspiration struck, though I don't remember whose. We rushed to buy several cartons of Frooti, a local fruit drink, for its sugar and orange concentrate. It provided crucial glucose, and we managed like this for six to seven agonising hours. The moment we disembarked in Bangalore, our first act was to admit him to a hospital. He was treated for dehydration and gastritis. We soon realised the culprit was green chillis in the previous night's dinner, a known trigger after his ulcer diagnosis and surgery, because of which Dad left the army. We were incredibly careful on subsequent trips, forever mindful of this harrowing journey that in its own way added a powerful albeit challenging, layer to our family's shared impact and memories.

Our next LTA trip was to Goa. Ironically, both my parents had yearned to visit Delhi, but destiny had other plans. This Goa trip, little did we know, would be Dad's last. He had famously ridden a friend's Yezdi motorbike to Goa in the 1980s, a feat none of us have since replicated. When healthy and able, he truly savoured life. Perhaps that innate desire to travel, to explore, is now deeply embedded in our own memories. His health had begun to fluctuate, and increasing work pressure further diminished his physical fitness. Even a single glass of alcohol began to affect him profoundly, marking a poignant shift in the experiences we could share as a family.

Gradually, our family trips dwindled, and then, without much discussion, they simply ceased. Other priorities had asserted themselves. Yet, Mom was blessed to join a group of believers on a trip to Jerusalem. She wasn't alone, Prabhakar uncle, Linora aunt, and even my in-laws joined her. Mom would recount her experiences with such fervour, sharing her deep connection to that sacred place, the overwhelming feelings it evoked, and the way it solidified her faith. In stark contrast to that spiritual journey, one trip that holds a special place in my heart was our visit to Velankanni for my son Ben's second birthday. Three sisters (Doddamma, Chikkama and Mom), my in-laws, and cousin Anand's family, all came along. It was such a blessing to be surrounded by family who had been there for us during our formative years, continued to be present in our adulthood, and now shared in the joys of our children's lives. This continuum of family presence, through life's various stages, beautifully demonstrated how memories are built across generations. Being spiritual also pushes us towards certain rituals that we follow almost unknowingly, and visiting Velankanni was one such family ritual that most of us attended regularly.

Three sisters with Anand sitting in front of shrine of Velankanni

After Jerusalem, Mom embarked on more solo adventures, visiting Singapore and Auckland. She did one more trip and after that ceased traveling much. However, she would regularly visit Hyderabad, where Sudheer and Sheeba, who love hosting people, ensured every visitor explored the city and its surroundings. Mom managed to see most of these places.

Singapore visit

One of the most unforgettable memories for all of us was when Mom returned from Auckland. She missed her connecting flight to Bangalore in Singapore due to the late arrival of her flight to Singapore from Auckland. Imagine her situation, not a regular English speaker, with stiffness in her right hand and leg, no mobile phone, limited money, and travelling alone for the first time on a 20 hour flight. Yet, somehow, she managed. She spoke to strangers, sought help, found a translator to communicate with the airline staff, secured accommodation, and rebooked her flight for the next morning. Even she was astonished by her own resourcefulness.

Maori stories were very interesting for her and she couldn't stop her excitement of taking a picture with Maori warriors

As our parents age and we mature, it is common to assume we possess greater knowledge, sometimes offering unsolicited advice or questioning their wisdom. We may dismiss their experiences as relevant only to their generation, a tendency many of us share. Often, we overlook the emotional impact this has on them, as they may not express their hurt except through a quiet hope that we will understand when we encounter similar circumstances. This realisation has become a meaningful lesson, fostering humility and empathy within us.

Mt Eden, she was pleasantly surprised to see the crater

In today's generation, there is a deliberate effort to create memories through elaborate photoshoots, lavish birthday celebrations, extravagant and innovative weddings, and the growing trend of reunions, all designed to etch moments into our lives. In our case, however, the stage was set effortlessly for many years by communities, villages, extended families, and friends, and we shared truly wonderful times together. While our parents didn't intentionally orchestrate these opportunities, the society they lived in was inherently emotionally connected and inclusive. It stands in stark contrast to our world today, where connection often feels devoid of true emotion. Our parents lived simple lives with simple aspirations. They were inherently good to people. I have never, in my entire life, heard Dad raise his voice, privately or publicly. He never once struck his children. Even today, 23 years after his passing, his deeds resonate.

Mom at Iconic ECP beach in singapore

Even those who did not work directly with Dad acknowledge the significant influence of his actions, which extended well beyond his immediate circle. The same is true for Mom. I have often heard stories of children inspired to attend school after observing her dedication and perseverance, particularly her independence in riding a scooter. Their lives and experiences have provided us with a sense of purpose, demonstrating how to live and love meaningfully. Their legacy continues to enrich our lives, as they lived fully and left behind enduring memories that shape us.

While a kite represents our individual flight against the unpredictability of life, it is the weaving of our collective stories that provides us with lasting strength. The "Woven Lives" of our community and extended family, act as a protective fabric, far more resilient than a single sheet of kite paper. As we move from the solitary heights of our own journeys into the shared warmth of our family's history, we see that every challenge faced was merely a tension on the loom, tightening the bond between generations. We are the legacy of that careful weaving, a tapestry of memories that remains intact, long after the winds of struggle have died down.

CHAPTER 7

A LEGACY OF GRIT AND GRACE

Several months ago, my friends and I engaged in a thoughtful reflection on our lives between the ages of 35 and 45. We made considerable efforts to recall significant events beyond our immediate families. Yet, the more we tried, the fewer memorable moments we could identify. While a few friends, endowed with exceptional memories, could recount their experiences in detail, for most of us, that decade appeared indistinct, a reflection of how deeply absorbed we became in our careers, family responsibilities, and planning for the future. This period seemed to create a void where individual experiences faded. It is remarkable how we often focus so intently on preparing for the future that we neglect to appreciate the present.

Indian tradition conceptualises life as a progression through distinct phases, Brahmacharya (student), dedicated to learning and celibacy, Grihastha (householder), focused on family, work, and societal contribution, Vanaprastha (forest hermit), characterised by gradual detachment and spiritual pursuit, and Sanyasa (renunciate), marked by complete renunciation. Although these stages are not always strictly observed, they ideally delineate the human journey. Even when these distinctions are not precisely followed, the underlying trajectory of growth, responsibility, and eventual detachment remains prevalent for most people, friends, colleagues, relatives, and parents alike. This reflection centers on the shared, relatable human experience rather than on exceptional cases.

Mom and Dad in 1970s

It is only through experiencing these life phases that we come to understand the unique challenges each presents. Frequently, we share stories with our children, such as, "When I was studying engineering, it was so tough," or, "When I was your age, I used to do this." These anecdotes serve as reference points, helping to guide or illustrate lessons from our own past. However, questions arise when there is no such reference point and the path forward is entirely uncharted.

Pioneers of a New Dawn

My parents were thrust into exactly such a world. As first generation graduates, they were pioneers who stepped into roles that dismantled and redefined the societal norms of their small corner of the world. Imagine, in an era where education was a distant dream for many, Dad was the only person in about 14 surrounding villages to have passed his secondary school (SSLC/ 10th grade). Mom, too, achieved this remarkable milestone. This wasn't merely an academic achievement, it was, as I've heard, a rare qualification that made them "Eligible for Public Service" (EPS) a significant feat in their era, a golden ticket to a different kind of life.

It was especially uncommon during that era, particularly in rural areas, for both spouses to be employed, such an arrangement represented a significant departure from prevailing societal norms. At the time, men were generally expected to provide for the family, while women managed the household, ensured the family's welfare, and planned for the future. My parents, however, chose a different path. They occupied pioneering roles, frequently relocated due to work, nurtured ambitious dreams for their family, and continually adapted to new circumstances. Les Brown's statement, *"Life has no limitations, except the ones you make,"* could have served as their guiding principle, even before it was articulated. Their journey was marked by a determination to transcend conventional expectations and pursue new possibilities.

Farming to Family Endeavor

When our grandfather passed away, the idea of continuing his farming tradition was far from our minds. We, as children, had constantly heard that farming was no longer viable, it required more manpower, more money, and the precious water sources were dwindling. The nearby lake, our primary source of water, visibly receded each year, and the monsoons, once reliable life givers for crops, grew increasingly irregular. An open well that once held 3 to 4 meters of water throughout the year had gone down to just a couple of feet, which was insufficient. My grandfather, who once cultivated a commercial crop alongside food grains annually, had slowly and reluctantly shifted to growing only non commercial, low value crops like ragi millet, paddy, popcorn, and groundnut primarily for family consumption. There were times when he grew more lucrative crops like sugarcane, watermelon, beans, pulses, and sunflowers, but those days seemed long past. He was aging, his energy and health no longer able to withstand the relentless demands of full time agriculture. We also had local cows (Hallikar breed, one of the best draught breeds of southern India) for farming and milk. My grandmother, ever resourceful, kept chicken, sheep, goats, and later buffaloes, selling milk for revenue.

Agriculturalists, in our fields

When my parents, firmly established in their government service careers, decided to take on farming as a side hustle, we had no idea how profoundly it would change our lives forever. Suddenly, we, the children, found ourselves working in the fields, a novel experience for us. During Grandfather's time, we did it for fun, which later proved handy for helping our parents. Mom, with no prior farming knowledge, was bitten by the farming bug, an unexpected passion taking root. Dad, however, had farming in his blood, he'd worked the land until he joined the military, and even during his annual holidays, he would inevitably return to the fields, drawn by an invisible pull.

Confronted with ongoing water shortages, my parents, demonstrating resourcefulness, invested a significant portion of their savings to drill a borewell. Unable to manage daily agricultural tasks due to their professional commitments, they employed others to oversee the farm. While this approach was common among working families seeking development, for us, it marked the beginning of a transformative experiment. Our family became actively engaged in a local agricultural shift, persistently challenging ourselves over months and years.

In the villages surrounding us, farming was an instinct, a default setting for the soul. It didn't matter what a person's 'official' title was, teachers, doctors, bank employees, engineers, and local politicians all shared a second life in agriculture. While their primary jobs provided the revenue for daily survival, the land was where they sustained the community. Our grandfather for many years did not buy any groceries as there was a barter system within the village. Even when we started farming, for a few years, we didn't have to buy a single grain. Our land gave us everything: lentils, millet, rice, and peanuts, a direct harvest from our own toil. Different types of greens and lentils, plucked fresh, were cooked and served.

The financial outcomes of the farm fluctuated considerably. Occasionally, positive returns validated my parents' efforts and investments. At other times, breaking even provided a sense of relief. However, losses occurred frequently, serving as difficult reminders of the inherent risks associated with agriculture.

My parents were navigating uncharted territory, they lacked a clear reference point for this complex, hands off owner model. Dad's only blueprint for farming was his own father and relatives, men whose lives were defined by having their hands physically in the soil from dawn until dusk. Now, our parents were managing others to do that work for them, a completely different and difficult dynamic.

This new phase introduced additional challenges that required greater time and energy from my parents. As demands increased, they involved us, their children, in the farming activities. Although we did not particularly enjoy the labor and lacked the dedication, we participated out of a sense of family responsibility. In doing so, we became active participants in a cycle we had previously only observed.

Agriculture became a central, consuming focus in our family. We even had close friends in the Agriculture department who provided invaluable advice, their technical expertise guiding our parents. We transitioned from non commercial crops to more lucrative commercial ones. Tomatoes were a widespread trend among farmers, creating a vibrant red carpet across the landscape, followed by the lush green of beans, then cabbage, popcorn, and groundnut in a relentless cyclical pattern. With technical support from specialists, our parents simply "followed the yellow line," their trust in expert guidance unwavering. Our weekends and holidays, once reserved for leisure, became synonymous with farming tasks, whether it was watering, weeding, planting, or harvesting.

This new venture brought its own set of trials, none more persistent than the power issues that plagued our irrigation. Despite the demands of his day job, Dad would often venture out into the dead of night to water the crops, his flashlight beam cutting a lonely path through the darkness. On one of those unfortunate nights, the vulnerability of the land turned into a nightmare, he was mugged and robbed of his salary, watch, and gold ring. It was a devastating blow that left my parents struggling to manage the family's needs for months afterwards.

The labor didn't end with the harvest. Packing and selling the produce was a grueling, meticulous task. At times, we sold directly from the farm to save on transportation, but more often, we took the harder path. We would pack every crate ourselves, load them onto a truck, and embark on a 200 kilometer journey to Anantapur, a major market in the neighbouring state. While the strategy was exhausting, it allowed us to bypass the ubiquitous middlemen and bring home a better return.

For us, then in our teens, these journeys were a formative paradox. There was a sense of raw adventure in riding through the night for six hours with the villagers, watching the world blur by from the back of a truck. We witnessed the frantic, early morning drama of the vegetable market, the shouting, the deals, the constant motion. But we also saw the darker side, the unwelcoming experiences, the sight of highway accidents, and the crushing financial losses that came when a late arrival meant our produce had lost its value.

We experienced these events as they unfolded, becoming integral to the process. Those years strengthened us physically, mentally, and in our understanding of the world. The intensity of these challenges may explain why none of us pursued agriculture as a profession. Even when Sudheer graduated from agricultural college, he remained distant from farming on our land to this day. While we appreciated the rewards of the harvest, we also understood the significant hardships involved.

A Home Filled with Love and Life

Despite the demands of farming, our home maintained a comforting and stable environment, providing respite from daily challenges. My parents, particularly Mom and Sudheer, were passionate about animals, a sentiment that shaped our household. We always had dogs, pigeons, chickens, and an aquarium that captivated us, although the goldfish rarely survived. Pigeons remained for years, and dogs were a constant presence.

A special, almost unspoken bond existed between Mom and the dogs, deepened by Sudheer's shared affection. Mom was incredibly kind to them, and they seemed to instinctively know who was the "boss" at home, recognising her gentle authority. When she lived with me in Bangalore, we had a large German shepherd dog (Caesar), and later a smaller, more playful one, Pomeranian (Five-turn). Sudheer had a midsized mixed breed, Scooby. She doted on them, taking them for walks, feeding them on time, cooking separate meals tailored to their needs, and ensuring they were bathed regularly.

Each of us gained distinct formative experiences through farming. Sharath developed a strong connection to agriculture and remained involved until recent years. He also understands issues and challenges of owning revenue lands. Sudheer's professional work in agricultural research for a multinational corporation also linked him to agriculture, and his expertise provided valuable insights, even if not always directly applicable to our small scale operations. Farming persisted even after Dad's passing, reflecting his enduring influence, but gradually diminished as Mom retired and our family relocated to Bangalore. Although Mom wished to continue, increasing challenges led us to withdraw from farming over time.

A School is Born

A new and profound passion emerged within our family, fundamentally redefining our collective purpose. Mom, inspired by an unmissable opportunity, committed herself wholeheartedly to a venture deeply meaningful to her. This marked the start of a challenging yet rewarding 15 year journey that required immense energy and dedication. Our family, both intentionally and inadvertently, embarked on its next significant endeavor, education. The decision to establish an English medium school in a rural community, initially proposed by Sudarshan uncle, became a reality through Mom's steadfast commitment. She approached this new chapter with enthusiasm and resilience.

My parents hailed from families where formal education was a distant dream. Both of their parents worked for missionaries and a mission run hospital, serving as butlers and working in close proximity to doctors and administrators. From childhood, my parents observed the British, marvelling at how they spoke English with effortless grace and watching their children diligently study from "big, big books" that seemed like symbols of an entirely different world.

When Mom passed her 8th grade (LS), the missionaries, recognising her sharp intelligence, advised my grandparents to send her directly into nurse training. However, my grandparents and Mom remained resolute, she would finish her 10th grade before pursuing any vocational training, a testament to their foresight and her own quiet ambition. This foundation of education eventually led them to a bold new venture that filled the family with excitement, starting their own school.

I was not directly involved in the school initiative. Being away from home, I found it difficult to fully grasp the vision. I questioned the feasibility of the project, doubting whether villagers could afford the required fees and whether we could recruit teachers who met my parents' standards for quality education. Unexpected logistical challenges soon arose, such as the villagers' demand for transportation, which shifted the management's focus from education to organising daily commutes. Managing transportation became a new responsibility. My critical perspective during this period created tension and distanced me from the family's central activities more than I had anticipated. I was proven wrong, the school grew rapidly by the quality of the education provided, commitment and more than that the credibility of Mom and Dad.

A School function

Dad was the only son among five siblings, his sisters studied only until about 8th grade, a common stopping point for girls of their generation. For my grandfather, who had transitioned from butler work to village farming, ensuring all his children studied was a monumental task, a constant struggle against limited resources. Dad, understanding the profound importance of education, persevered against the odds and passed his 10th grade. He began teaching in a school, working alongside my Jayamama, also a teacher. Then, the undeniable call of the country beckoned, and

Dad, with a quiet determination, chose to join the army. I still don't fully understand how this unfolded, probably my parents have told me about that, I don't remember. We had no family members in the army before him, and our grandparents lived far from any cantonment or army camp. Our village had no one in the army. Born in pre-independent India in 1943, he would have experienced the exhilaration of India's freedom from the British from a very young age.

In the initial days of the school, they did not have the building but had the will to do all that is required.

Education played a transformative role in my parents' lives, guiding them toward opportunities previously unavailable to their families. This influence ensured that my siblings and I attended reputable schools at every level. My parents aspired for us not only to graduate but to become professionals capable of adapting to a rapidly changing world. Their ambitions for us were shaped by their own experiences and observations. For them, agriculture became a supplementary activity rather than a primary focus. Coming from a lineage without formal educators, they were determined to ensure that future generations would be well educated and able to overcome limitations.

To send their children to private and English medium schools, they made immense, silent sacrifices. Such schools weren't available locally, requiring us to endure a grueling hour long commute each way. They quickly realised the impracticality and the immense expense of sending their children to schools so far away, not only for us but also for the children in the village. This was why most likely, when Sudarshan uncle, a visionary in his own right, proposed starting an English school, our parents enthusiastically endorsed the idea. After brief, passionate deliberations, they agreed to open the school in Peresandra in 1998, a decision that would change the trajectory of countless young lives.

School office

It was a completely new world for all of us, especially for Sharath, Mom, and our uncles. While the entire family invested their precious time and effort, some poured in more than they ever thought possible, driven by a shared vision. Challenges were abundant, no one in the family had any experience of setting up a school, (though they were all teachers and understood the mechanics of running schools. Qualified teachers were scarce, student enrollment was low, and there was no proper building, just a dream taking shape on bare land. Sudarshan uncle had experience of starting a church school in a city and was a mentor for this core group. It was a pioneering effort, aiming for the highest standards in education, a beacon of hope in a village yearning for progress. It was difficult, undoubtedly, but not impossible. Dad, primarily an observer in this new venture, provided invaluable administrative consulting, his calm wisdom a guiding force. The day to day administration, however, was largely handled by Mom, Sharath, Smitha and Sudarshan uncle. They endured countless sleepless nights, huddled over plans, meticulously organising, and implementing best practices gleaned from their own teaching experience. Like any other startup venture, even here, there was always demand for funds, resources, and skills. For the first couple of years, money was scarce, so the teachers in our family did not take any wages to support the cause.

As the school progressed, the first year was a triumphant hurdle, Smitha, Sheeba, and Sweety joined as teachers, providing a much needed breather for the administrators to ensure seamless classroom operations. Mom no longer had to double up as a teacher, juggling it with her regular government work and administrative duties, a burden finally lifted.

Several aspects of our lives were developing simultaneously. My siblings and I were focused on building our professional careers, while agriculture continued to occupy our time and remind us of our heritage. The establishment of the school introduced an additional layer of complexity and responsibility. Our family's primary motivation was to provide quality education to village children, sparing them the difficulties we had faced, such as long commutes and limited access. As the school expanded, so did the associated challenges and responsibilities. Importantly, the school also generated employment for several family members and local residents, supporting the community and exemplifying the tangible benefits of our family's pioneering efforts. The fulfillment derived from vidhyadanam, or the gift of education, was profound, and the school's rapid growth reflected our collective dedication.

New School building inauguration

Concurrently, a couple of corporate schools with substantial investments began to sprout up in the village, their shiny facades contrasting with our more humble beginnings. While competition is often good for business, here it was a clash between a deeply rooted, service oriented mindset and a slick, corporate one. Sustaining a service model against the sheer financial might of corporate investment proved challenging, yet Mom never gave up. After Dad passed away, all her immense energy, her very essence, started flowing into her work and the school. She was vibrant, motivated, and eager to do whatever it took to nurture her "baby". She would take leave from her regular job, sacrificing her own comfort, to step in and teach when some teachers failed to show up. She was, quite simply, one of the best administrators at work, at home, at school, or within the family. Gifted with an uncanny ability to multitask, she could quickly assess situations and find solutions without wasting a single precious moment. She would sit for hours, meticulously preparing for teaching, consulting numerous references to give the children the most accurate, insightful information. Indeed, she was an avid reader in her younger years, devouring novels daily, her mind constantly seeking knowledge. She would carry library books to work, reading them on the bus, while waiting for the bus, during breaks, or even after dinner. Her moments were never dull or lethargic. Even from her childhood, she was very creative, she read books in Telugu and translated them to Kannada, she used to sit for hours watching nature, and draw what she was enjoying. While she kept herself busy, she also ensured we read books. I, too, was bitten by the reading bug, eagerly devouring weekly magazines, Women's Era, and books from the library. This is probably when I picked up Telugu (one of the South Indian languages), reading and immersing myself in the rich narratives of Maladi and Yaddanapudi Sulochanarani. Dad, loyal to Prajavani, a daily newspaper, also found solace in Lankesh Patrike, a political satire weekly, each finding their own intellectual nourishment.

Twists of Fate and Unspoken Voids

Life takes unexpected twists and turns, often without warning. Priorities shift, focus changes, and competition intensifies. Our family, with its deeply ingrained service oriented approach, simply couldn't compete with the massive investments of the corporate schools. This inevitable truth led to a gradual decrease in student enrollment, a painful reality after so much effort. With age and the shifting priorities of Mom, she had to gradually step back from the school, passing the responsibility to Smitha and Sharath, a torch reluctantly passed.

Growing older brought its own set of challenges for Mom, health issues began to surface, the raw grief of Dad's demise, the subtle shift in power dynamics as her children grew into adults with their own opinions, her quiet loss of control over what she had flawlessly managed for so long, coupled with the inevitable attainment of retirement age. While she presented a brave face to the world, a stoic mask for those around, I often wondered about the silent suffering she endured, the weight of a life lived for others. While her children were well settled, having benefited immensely from her instrumental role in their 18 years of education, and despite her brave venture into agriculture, there still seemed to be something missing in her eyes, a quiet void. She retired in 2006 and dedicated herself fully to the school, a final act of devotion, though her heart yearned to spend time with her precious grandchildren growing up in Bangalore. We, her children, didn't fully comprehend the complex emotions swirling in her mind at that time, but she poured her boundless love into her two grandsons, Ben and Alan.

Ben, Anna and Alan with Mom.

She meticulously planned and invested in their names more than me and Sharath did, a testament to her profound affection. She would buy them toys, dresses, and even gold, always two sets, Ben and Alan were truly her "two eyes," the light of her life. She had always longed for a daughter and believed her third child would be a girl, but God had other plans. When we, her sons, also had no daughters, it became a quiet, lingering sadness. One of her biggest voids, a heartache that never fully healed, is Sudheer and Sheeba not having their own children, again God's inscrutable plans. When her grandchildren started going to school, she was overjoyed, a radiant happiness filling her, knowing she had helped countless parents in the village provide a good education for their children, easing their burdens.

With Alan and Ben

Across cultures, blessings are often believed to be transmitted through generations. The decades of dedicated service, sacrifice, and integrity demonstrated by our parents continue to benefit our family, providing a sense of protection and continuity. Even years after their passing, their reputation for integrity and selflessness endures in the community. We recognise that our current circumstances are a direct result of their efforts, and we remain deeply grateful for these enduring blessings.

Mom's last day of work

Send-off from her staff and peers

Perhaps we gave our parents some satisfaction, though not as much to Dad, who didn't spend much time with us after we grew up and settled. We often heard that Dad would brag about us, his pride bursting, even before we had achieved anything close to what they had accomplished despite their immense constraints. Mom used to tell us that Dad would discuss each of our individual natures and qualities with her, as if he already knew the adults we would become. When he was tipsy, a rare loosening of his strict composure, he would sometimes share profound life advice with us, guiding us on what to do and what not to do. Mom always said that Dad was incredibly proud of us, a quiet source of joy for her. We heard similar sentiments about her from our uncles, aunts, and her cherished friends, a chorus of admiration for her strength and love. While they provided us with the bedrock of education, they also ensured we remained grounded, instilling strong values, to be kind and respectful to others, and never to cause harm. They were wonderfully naive, profoundly sincere, and beautifully simple people. All they asked was to be heard, or to be listened to in the moment, with calm explanations offered once their initial emotions had cooled. Though Mom was quite short tempered during those incredibly stressful days, she underwent a remarkable transformation, evolving into a cool and calm person as she got older, her wisdom growing with her years. She clearly understood how we were behaving and parenting, and while she had all the freedom to talk and control us, she wisely suggested the right thing to do, never dictating, always guiding.

Reflections on Love and Family

Our parents' togetherness, their enduring friendship, their willingness to compromise, to let go of minor grievances, and their incredible adjusting nature taught us meaningful life lessons, keeping our relationships intact to this day.

Glowing together

Even as grown ups living independent lives, we still deeply respect their togetherness, their openness, their unwavering support for each other, and the way they ensured life continued, no matter the obstacle. We need to be thankful for God's blessing in giving us such parents, and equally, for giving us the best partners in our individual lives who have built this family, supported their husbands, and kept this great legacy going, flourishing with each generation.

Our parents also had their share of in-law experiences. Dad didn't quite enjoy father-in-lawhood, it was a new experience, often a perplexing dynamic for him.

Dad with granny and Dad's sister.

Since our parents didn't have a girl child, they were overjoyed to have three beautiful girls at home. But with that happiness, the complex realities of in-law relationships truly kicked in. The world they knew, and their deeply held expectations, didn't always align with the new dynamics, leading to inevitable friction. Like any other family, it was a challenging time for all of us. It took a long time to understand how each individual was, their unique personalities, and their ways of being. Eventually, either side reached a point of quiet acceptance and said, "It's okay," adopting a way to live without constant clashes. Mom quickly learned to agree to disagree, sometimes standing firm, sometimes giving up, but crucially, never complaining to her children about the fights and arguments with the daughter-in-laws, protecting us from their disagreements. The girls (daughter-in-law), too, did the same. They didn't spread negativity, keeping matters to themselves, only informing their better halves if something was noticeably different or truly needed attention. Smitha spent the most time with Mom, a quiet presence by her side, and she has probably taken over the mantle in the family, continuing to keep everyone together, a quiet, strong force.

Mom shared an exceptional, profound bond with her grandchildren. While she had opportunities to build relationships with our cousins' children, it was for a limited time, few fleeting moments. But when Ben was born in 2004 and Alan in 2006, she burst into tears, tears of overwhelming joy. There were no words to explain her happiness. She was incredibly fond of Ben and Alan, her heart overflowing, and ensured that they were cared for precisely as she desired, a meticulous devotion. While she stayed in Bangalore, she would jump to cook even before Ben asked for something, anticipating his every need. She would know what he would eat and have it cooked or kept ready for him when he came back from school. Her life did change, her interests changed, and her desire for control shifted. While she loved her grandchildren a lot, she also wanted to keep them in her orbit, under her gentle influence. We all know how children are, they take the best from all that's available, embracing boundless love. She told them countless stories, read them stories from beloved books, played with them, her laughter echoing with theirs. She shielded them, supported them, and gave them generously, without reservation. Wherever she went, whatever she bought, it had to be for her grandchildren first, then others. I had never seen her so possessive, so fiercely devoted to anyone, not even to us, her own children. Her favourite son was Sudheer, and Sharath was Dad's. Even when they grew up, they took sides, and I think probably I do too. While we were young, she was busy designing life for us, she was running all the time and hardly had time to pamper us like she wanted to and make us feel special.

Grandfather with us.

With regard to her in-law relationships, she did not have a great bond. While they had their moments and shared experiences, it never grew into something deeper. Dad's sisters and Mom had a bit of closeness, spats, and misunderstandings. In patches, it was okay, but when needed, perhaps the support wasn't truly there. Coming from a large family of nine siblings to a family of five siblings, one might have expected it to be simple and easy, but relationships are rarely simple. When things were going well, they were very happy, sharing happiness, sadness, and even bitterness. While Dad was around, the relationship with our paternal aunts and their families was okay, we were very close with some of our cousins and genuinely enjoyed their company. However, our aunts and Mom could not reconcile after Dad passed, a quiet rift that widened over time. We saw our paternal aunts and their children now and then, but there was neither warmth nor hostility with them, just a fading connection between families. Our granny shuttled between our place and our aunts', taking turns, continuing to stay more with aunts. Mom always had strong feelings about it, she wanted to take care of my granny, but circumstances made it difficult. She supported her by sending granny money regularly, a small piece of comfort she could offer given the situation.

When considering questions such as, "What more could have been done?", the answers are often complex and difficult. Human nature inclines us to believe we could have overcome every obstacle, yet life unfolds unpredictably. We can only learn from past experiences, adopt the positive qualities observed in our parents, and strive to let go of ego and longstanding grievances. Letting go, especially within families, is challenging because of the expectations and emotional bonds involved. In a joint family system, the belief that one can influence siblings and their families often complicates relationships. Many family members were self made, which sometimes fostered strong opinions and judgments. In middle and low income families, self respect and a desire for control often emerge as byproducts of circumstance. Elders typically assume responsibility as parents age, guiding the family's direction. While this approach was not inherently wrong, it may have motivated our parents to strive for progress, whether as a challenge, a matter of survival, or a desire for a better life.

The Enduring Legacy of Grit

In every phase of their lives, we can see the sheer grit in our parents. Mom wanting to study and then pursuing staff nurse training, Dad leaving a stable teacher's job and going to the military to serve the country. They didn't stop there. They continued their fight as a family, whether it was enduring 13 transfers in 20 years, Mom courageously learning to ride a scooter when there was no example of a woman doing so in the villages, dreaming big and building a grand home, resolutely deciding to get a good education for their children, or constantly surpassing their own goals and their own exacting standards. This relentless drive, however, did not make them arrogant, they remained humble, always grounded, always ready to help and support each other. Our uncles and aunts were also experiencing and growing in a similar society with similar challenges, everyone striving to make ends meet, their own battles fought in the shadows. Life, often, is profoundly unfair.

"Midlife crisis" is a popular term in the modern age. Perhaps in my parents' generation, in their relentless pursuit of survival and betterment, they simply didn't have the luxury of time to think about such a crisis. Today, however, despite having more comfort and opportunity, we often find ourselves in a different kind of turmoil. We are in a relentless race, everyone young and old, a furious dash for success be it in our professions, in life, or within the family. At school, one needs to do well to get better grades. If one gets better grades, do they get to choose what to do with their higher studies? We must do well there too, to secure placements. Life feels boxed and stressed all the time, a constant pressure cooker.

In our parents' time, it was more about simply getting better than what we were before, whether in education, social stature, career, or ensuring a comfortable life upon retirement. Dad had a clear pathway in his career, though there weren't many promotions in his specific role. It was more about the position he would get by working in bigger and better offices. Working in the head office and being called a Head Postmaster was a significant achievement for him, a symbol of his dedication. At the pinnacle of his career, he headed around ten offices, along with an equal number of sub-offices, managing the daily rotation of large sums of cash. He was, in effect, at the helm of nearly 200 employees under that head office. He had worked very hard for that, never straying to the wrong side of the system or people. For him, work was worship, this may have come from his military experience. He was the first one to reach the office with keys in his pocket and the last one to lock the office, a true embodiment of dedication. Dad, being a simple and highly disciplined person, was not able to grow up amidst the politics around him. While there were no challenges in his role delivery, there were always challenges due to senior management's interference causing rifts in the office, a common, painful reality.

This unyielding moral compass of his was ironically creating problems for him at the office. He could not tolerate the constant friction of politics clashing with his principled stand. He was dragged closer to alcohol and gradually got used to it, a coping mechanism for the unbearable stress. It is not that he would go and get drunk every day. When Sharath went to college, and when they returned back home together, nothing would happen on those days. Briefly, when Asha was working in Chikkaballapur, and she would go to the post office, and Dad would finish work around 5:30 p.m. and they would head home to Peresandra. Nothing would happen on those days either. But on some of those days when things went wrong, and he was with his company of friends, even with two pegs of whisky, he used to get tipsy and pass out, a public display which we thought brought shame to the family. Alcohol consumption was creating a disturbance in the family, a person with that stature being passed out in the public is something we as sons and Mom were not able to digest. We were worried about our respect and our dignity. We children, in a strange twist of youthful self absorption, thought that he was tarnishing our dignity, which was strange in hindsight. I have often reflected with regret on my behaviour during those times. It was so funny that we were born to him, and we were teaching him how to live. A person who had seen the world, he just smiled as a response. None of us gave him the comfort that he probably was looking for or wanted, the gentle understanding he craved. It was his office crisis that he took to heart, yet he never showed it outwardly. He tried a couple of times to give up alcohol. He went to a de-addiction center, which helped offer a glimmer of hope, but it did not fully resolve the issue. During our trip to Goa, where spirits flow freely, he did not drink a single drop of alcohol. Later on, he reduced his drinking outside. As a member of the military canteen, he could buy good whiskey, which he kept discreetly in the cupboard. He would have a single peg before the weekend lunch and then quietly sleep it off. This became his practice after he took a simpler work assignment away from the head office and began leading a more comfortable life.

During his time, he had multiple health issues. Three heart attacks, a devastating accident that fractured his leg, the profound loss of his own Dad, spats with some of his close friends, and the ever present complexities of the home situation. He balanced it all very well most of the time, though a certain phase of life had affected his mental well-being, leaving behind invisible wounds from a life fully lived. Had he lived to see us come into our own, I like to imagine him finally savoring the quiet luxuries he was so often denied, an exotic drink, a meal prepared without the sting of spice, or the simple joy of a new journey. We feel his absence most acutely now that we have the means to honor him. We missed the chance to buy him that drink, to dress him in the clothes he admired, or to take him to the far-off places he had only ever dreamed of visiting. We carry the bittersweet weight of being able to provide everything he lacked, yet having no way to give it to him. But such is life, we don't always have solutions, because it is life, and life simply happens, with all its beautiful, painful, and often inexplicable turns.

Mom too had her share of profoundly personal challenges, battles fought close to her heart. When she started driving her scooter, embracing a newfound independence, navigating the dusty roads between villages to serve people, she had to endure nasty comments and pointed whispers. But she didn't bother much, as Vasundra, Radhamani, Savithramma, Channapa, Anand Murthy, along with Dad, formed her unwavering support system. At home, she had Vasanthamma, Prabhumama, Jayamama, who played an important role by offering their support. Lots was going on in her life, a constant whirlwind of activity, that she barely had time to dwell on anything beyond her immediate family or the demands of her work. She was undeniably a go-getter and a doer, a highly ambitious and determined person, a woman of action, and she was able to pursue all of it because of the steadfast support of Dad and her siblings. Her bond with her family was great, in fact, we as children spent more time with Mom's siblings and cousins than with Dad's side, but these connections were largely buried under the weight of daily life. She had her share of fights, compromises, commitments, collaborative efforts, and partnerships in investments, navigating the complexities of family finances with astute dedication.

She was very close with her elder brothers initially, and later on, her bond with her younger brothers and sisters strengthened, a natural evolution of relationships. She was the fifth of nine siblings, four older and four younger, nestled in the middle, forming particularly close bonds with her elder sister Ruthamma and her younger sister Vasanthamma. While they didn't meet regularly, as each of them was sinking and swimming in their own lives, much like Mom, but they shared a great, unspoken bond. Even after Mom became a grandmother, she was still, almost reverently, "scared" of her elder sister, a respect born not of dread, but of admiration. I never saw them argue, or at least, I don't remember it. In the case of her younger sister, however, she had her share of spirited fights. It was a classic trait of Mom that she simply did not build grudges with her family and friends.

Brothers and sisters

Everyone faces challenges in life, and few are born into privilege. We each have aspirations and work diligently to achieve them, often with success. However, as time passes, we may reflect on unrealised potential and unused talents, questioning whether we have fully utilised our abilities.

These talents could range from culinary skills to scientific innovation, engineering, endurance, or creative pursuits. The essential question is whether we are making the most of our capabilities or allowing circumstances to limit us. My parents dreamed ambitiously and achieved much, often forging new paths and encouraging us to do the same. While it is easy to suggest more could have been accomplished, many are constrained by their circumstances. Nevertheless, we have the opportunity to contribute meaningfully to our own lives and to society. My parents never succumbed to self-pity or victimhood, instead, they focused on action and determination. They improved our standard of living, instilled strong values, and ensured our family's upward mobility. Most importantly, they encouraged us to reflect, learn, and live fully, leaving a legacy of both achievement and generosity.

The story of the school and the farm is not merely one of business, but of a sacred stubbornness. It is the story of a Mom who became "Scooter Madam" to outrun the limitations of her era, and a Dad who stood in the darkness of a midnight field because the land was his "instinct for the soul." They bore the "sting of social condescension" and the "crushing financial losses" of the market, not as defeats, but as the price of our freedom.

We realise that the "void" they left wasn't an absence, but a space they cleared for us to grow. By turning their sweat into our degrees and their sacrifices into our stability, they ensured that our family tapestry would never again be frayed by the lack of a "permanent address." Their legacy is the quiet knowledge that while the monsoons may be irregular and the corporate facades may rise, a life rooted in Vidhyadanam, the gift of education, will forever remain in bloom.

CHAPTER 8
THE QUIET ARCHITECT

We often discuss success, recalling the well-known saying that behind every successful man stands a woman. In our family, this principle is clearly demonstrated, our achievements, stability, and life paths are inseparably connected to one remarkable woman, the heart and soul of our home, who supported our needs and ambitions with unwavering dedication.

While Mom fulfilled her vital role as a beacon of service and dedication, an equally important presence shaped our family's foundation. Dad devoted himself entirely to our well-being, offering quiet support, balance, and encouragement, never seeking attention and becoming the protective structure under which we thrived.

Mid 1980s, Sharath in the middle

Dad guided our family behind the scenes, shaping individual lives, aspirations, and shared experiences. With a distinct style, steady pace, and humility, he embodied simplicity. Avoiding complexity and grand strategies, he preferred direct action. Though he spoke little, his actions demonstrated the impact of quiet leadership, and his unassuming nature earned the respect of all.

The insight of Rabindranath Tagore "It is very simple to be happy, but it is very difficult to be simple" held no difficulty for him. For him, simplicity and happiness were interchangeable.

Center of our lives

His character was formed in a unique environment. He grew up among five women, his Mom and four sisters in a small village of fewer than 500 people. He consistently demonstrated respect for women, whether in the community, workplace, or at home.

This humble background made it not just easy, but natural for him to be the unwavering support for his better half whenever the call of duty took her away. The nature of Mom's work in emergency services often took her away from home for days at a time, particularly during large scale efforts like the polio camps, family planning programs, eye camps, the leprosy eradication campaign, and many more.

During those absences Dad took on his own mission, caring for his three young "musketeers," along with our pets and birds. We were young, needy, and demanding of attention. He did it all patiently, without a single word of complaint or qualm. He was the cook, the cleaner, the one who bathed and dressed us, packed our lunches, went to work, and returned home only to begin the routine again. His satisfaction was clearly derived from the seamless running of the home. This ease with organisation and management came from the fact that such discipline was the norm for him, shaped by years of training and life in the army.

His unwavering commitment was most evident when Mom attended a year long training in Chitradurga in 1982. At that time, the youngest of us, Sudheer was seven, and I was twelve. Dad calmly assured us that he would manage both our care and his professional responsibilities.

Dad with his co-brothers, 1976

He exemplified discipline, maintaining order and routine in our lives. Remarkably, he never resorted to physical punishment or even raised his voice. While Mom sometimes used the cane for discipline, Dad never needed to. She often observed that we were more afraid of him, not because of overt threats, but due to the fear of disappointing his quiet trust. This subtle influence kept us disciplined, content, and secure.

We lived without television, so our lives revolved around playgrounds, friends, and each other. While in the training, Mom was visiting every month or two, our routine became both stretched and compressed. Her visits brought celebrations, with days of preparation before she departed again. At the time, we were too young to appreciate the complexity of Dad managing everything alone. Time passed without our awareness, as we simply lived within the stability he provided. Now, when Asha undertakes her training and certifications, immersing herself for weeks and leaving household tasks to Ben and me, I experience firsthand the challenges and frustrations. I realise I never saw such frustration in Dad, or perhaps he simply never showed it.

Hosted friends and family in our fields

Upon Mom's return, her promotion required frequent travel to major hospitals in Chikkaballapur and Kolar, as well as oversight of numerous PHCs (Public Health Centre) and Anganwadi (Early Child Education) centers. As her responsibilities increased, the balance at home needed adjustment, and Dad once again managed all household duties with characteristic grace and efficiency.

For the following decade, our family routine settled into a coordinated effort. Both parents rose early, completed all preparations, and left home by 8 a.m. with their lunches packed.

In 1993, Mom undertook a year long training in Dindigul, which was essential for her advancement to the highest position in her field. By then, we were older, living in Peresandra, and had household help, yet Dad remained the central figure at home. Sharath assumed greater responsibility, stepping in to manage the household as needed. With Sudheer in Bangalore and myself living and working elsewhere, this period became a special time for Dad and Sharath to bond and learn from each other, with Sharath developing notable cooking skills.

Sheeba's wedding ritual

Although we had become independent, Dad faced significant pressure at work, managing over 200 staff members at the Chikkaballapur office. This period revealed rare moments of vulnerability, as he shared the complex challenges he encountered. As a straightforward and honest individual, he lacked both the inclination and skill for office politics, making his integrity both a strength and a vulnerability. Later in his career, he developed a habit of drinking regularly due to work induced risk and stress. On occasion, even a modest quantity, about 60 ml of whisky would cause him to pass out. He avoided political maneuvering and did not seek recognition. He was a lifelong devotee of sports, though he favored Volleyball and Kabaddi, and later Cricket, his joy was found on the sidelines. He never stepped onto the field himself, yet he never missed a chance to witness the magic of the game. His true passion was for cerebral games like carroms and chess, where he excelled for the love of the game rather than competition. These games, rooted in skill and logic, suited him far more than the complexities of office politics.

His leisure time was uncomplicated yet fulfilling, listening to the news on radio or television, reading the newspaper thoroughly, and spending quiet moments with close friends over beedi and tea. Later, he added the quiet enjoyment of whisky to this routine.

The most lasting gifts he gave us were not material possessions, but values that serve as the foundation of our lives. Even now, when we visit his former workplace, it is gratifying to hear from those who never worked directly with him but know of his discipline and dedication. We feel deeply fortunate and grateful to be part of his family.

2001 Just before wedding for sudheer and sharath

2001 just after Marriage of Smitha and Sheeba

His daily routine was a masterclass in consistency, a steady rhythm that anchored our home. Every morning began with the rich, familiar scent of freshly brewed coffee. Sundays, however, held a different pace, he would immerse himself in the newspapers, enjoy a quiet beedi, and make his deliberate, ritualistic trip to the meat market.

The true essence of his life lay in this precise regularity. Like clockwork, at 10:30 a.m. he would shine his shoes and tidy the room with meticulous care. Lunch was always followed by a restorative nap, a pocket of calm he carved out amidst the day's demands. By 4 p.m. after his afternoon coffee, he would begin ironing the clothes for the week ahead. We stood beside him, following his silent example as we prepared our own school uniforms.

His return home each evening was as predictable and comforting as the sunset, signaling the transition to a simple dinner and a night of peaceful rest.

His professional values reflected his personal discipline. A sign on his office door read, "If you don't have a purpose here, don't stay," emphasising the importance of purposeful action. For him, discipline was transformative rather than burdensome. Whether addressing personal or professional matters, his solutions were grounded in simplicity and consistency. He was not a perfectionist, but rather deeply disciplined. His straightforward and pragmatic approach naturally earned the trust and respect of others.

This discipline is not merely a memory, it serves as the essential framework supporting our lives today.

We recognise that genuine support for our families is found not in grand gestures, but in consistent effort. We approach household responsibilities, emotional support, and childcare with the same dedication he demonstrated, enabling our partners to pursue their careers and passions without concern for the stability of our home.

In a world of over complication, his value of simplicity guides our daily choices. We eliminate clutter, both physical and mental, by applying his "no purpose, don't stay" rule to our routines, our goals, and our relationships. This prevents us from being consumed by the "noise" he always avoided.

We follow his example of prioritising action over words. When confronted with challenges at work or in life, our instinct is to implement simple, consistent, and direct solutions rather than engage in excessive planning.

His routine taught us more than any lecture could. We didn't learn the time from the clock's face, we learned it from his actions. His legacy is the powerful, quiet knowledge that success is built on a strong, consistent foundation.

Family picture we were all together for the last time Dec 2001

He was the person of unwavering character, the foundational strength of our family, and the driving force behind Mom's achievements. While it is often said that behind every successful man is a woman, it is equally true that a disciplined, simple, and devoted man can be the essential support behind a successful woman, creating a legacy that empowers his children to carry that strength forward.

Even today, I do not fully understand the depth of his strength or all his favorite things. I continue to seek the meaning behind his smile when we teased him, striving to comprehend his silence.

We often measure greatness by what a person "conquers," but this chapter measures it by what a person sustains. Dad's strength was not in a raised voice, but in a raised standard of care. He was a man who grew up surrounded by women and carried that deep-seated respect into his marriage, choosing to be the "wind beneath the wings" of a pioneering woman at a time when society rarely allowed men to play that role.

The profound truth here is that discipline is the highest form of devotion. He didn't just tell us how to live, he showed us the rhythm of his own life. He proved that a man's greatest legacy isn't the titles he earns at the office, but the peace he leaves in his home. His silence wasn't an absence, it was a presence so heavy and secure that his children never had to fear the world outside.

CHAPTER 9

UNFULFILLED DREAMS

We live in a world driven by instant gratification, where patience is diminishing. One hour deliveries are standard in many countries, in some places, food or groceries arrive within 10 to 15 minutes. I recall being genuinely surprised by such immediate services.

However, unmet expectations can cause profound disappointment. In April 2025, we ordered a cake for a significant birthday, scheduled for 10 p.m. but it never arrived. Our evening was overshadowed by frustration, and we directed our anger towards the mobile app and supplier.

A similar pattern emerges during carefully organised events, catering, decorating, inviting guests, and preparing with anticipation. We feel joy when attendees arrive, yet often our attention unconsciously shifts to the absence of one individual. We rationalise their absence, repeatedly check our phones, and inadvertently neglect those present. This reveals a difficult truth, we often fail to appreciate those who are present, focusing instead on what is missing.

This preoccupation with unmet expectations often recurs throughout life. We rarely dwell on the remarkable places we've visited, certifications earned, or achievements celebrated. Instead, unfulfilled dreams persist in our thoughts, reminding us of perceived shortcomings. The burden intensifies when we realise we could have helped someone achieve a dream but did not. We justify inaction with "we tried our best," "circumstances were beyond control," or "it was not in their destiny." We may postpone saying, "we'll do it next time," yet when is that next time? Opportunities may never return. I once promised to take Mom to see the snow in Auckland, but she never returned. Such unfulfilled wishes, especially for loved ones, can linger and cause lasting regret.

The Unspoken Language of Regret

Our family has its own share of unfulfilled dreams. While some aspirations were realised and may have altered the course of our lives, others could have fundamentally changed our perspectives and behaviours.

In Mom's case, she served over 40 years in the health department, and her ultimate goal was to see one of her children pursue medicine and become a doctor. She could never become a doctor herself, and she believed that with a doctor among us, we could care for society's well-being. Our parents were even willing to sell our property to put me through medical school, but I was not interested. Later, I realised that I couldn't bear the sight of blood, I would get stressed or faint. With my short temper and fainting spells, I would have made an awful doctor, perhaps doing more harm than good. When my brothers passed their preuniversity exams, she hoped Sudheer would become a doctor, but he chose an agricultural degree, to feed people, while Sharath became a civil engineer.

Our parents also wished to visit Delhi, Agra, and Jaipur. At one point, Dad traveled to Jaipur with a friend from Gudibande but did not continue on to Delhi or Agra. They admired national leaders and wanted to visit memorials, including India Gate, to honor those who had laid down their lives for the nation. Having served in the military himself, Dad had immense respect for all who served the nation.

When I once asked what would have happened if he had not returned from the military, he replied, "You would have joined the army too." Plans to visit Delhi and Agra arose several times, but we were not ready. As children, our focus was on education and building our home. Later, employment took precedence over travel. Even when we had the means, our own priorities delayed these trips. After 2002, we never explicitly decided against traveling, but life intervened, and our last family trip was to Goa. Mom lived for another 15 years, never complaining, yet the unfulfilled wish remained. We did not fully understand our parents' desires, nor did they voice disappointment.

There were also dreams that, we did not wish to fulfill. Living in a village, we often traveled to Chikkaballapur for gatherings, functions, or church events. The last bus departed at 8:45 p.m., requiring us to leave before most events concluded. After functions, while others returned to their homes in Chikkaballapur, we stayed with relatives. As we grew older, certain comforts became increasingly important for our parents, who also desired more time together. Mom even considered renting a place in Chikkaballapur but ultimately did not proceed. When an opportunity arose, she was determined to have a home in Chikkaballapur, perhaps to be on par with her siblings and friends or simply to have a place of her own in town. Despite frequent travel to Chikkaballapur for work and family, we opposed the idea, primarily due to concerns about cost and practicality, fearing it would create a conflict between the family home and a new residence. I now recognise that such a place would have benefited our parents, providing proximity to hospitals, improved living conditions, and social fulfillment. As a family, we did not support her in purchasing even a small plot of land in Chikkaballapur, fearing future obligations. We considered only our own perspectives, not hers, overlooking the frustration and disappointment she must have felt. Although she acquired land in Bangalore and took pride in our progress, her wish for a home in Chikkaballapur remained unfulfilled because of our decisions. To this day, none of us own a property there, and we attribute this outcome to destiny.

Mom had one more dream, to see real snow firsthand. Though she had seen ice from ice makers, and visited aquariums where penguins were near snow, she longed for natural snowfall, snow covered mountains, and trails. In India, we never went to Shimla or Darjeeling. Dad had lived in Darjeeling, Siliguri, Assam, and Calcutta, experiencing snow, but not Mom. She was drawn to the beauty of nature she saw in movies and visualised in books. In 2015, she had the opportunity to visit Auckland during winter, perfect for Mount Ruapehu. Before reaching Ruapehu, we drove to Cape Reinga, but I experienced nausea and lightheadedness along the way. Fortunately, a friend stepped in to help us. As we got closer to Ruapehu, I had another episode that forced us to postpone the trip, telling ourselves we would do it next time. I am reminded of this every time I see snow-covered mountains.

She also wished for Sharath, Smitha, Sudheer, Sheeba, and Alan to visit New Zealand and experience its beauty. Fortunately, that dream was realised in 2019. Through these experiences, I learned that the present moment is most valuable and within our control. Pursuing happiness today is essential, it should not be postponed for an uncertain future.

Cape Rianga, north tip of New Zealand

In this unpredictable and fragile life, anything might happen at any time, priorities might change, life might shift. Our postponements can create an irreparable void in life. It can be as simple as delaying a heartfelt apology to someone, putting off a reconciliation, or neglecting to answer a phone call from parents, spouse, children, family or friends. It can be about failing to spend quality time with family and friends, not trying to learn something we've always wanted to learn, or not inventing something we've always dreamed of creating. If some of these dreams depend on our support, or if we have the responsibility to fulfill them for our loved ones, what if we don't? Do we simply have to live with guilt, or what do we learn from such situations?

Checking out Bunker

Living Rich, Dying Poor in Regret

We bear the burden of unfulfilled dreams, both of our own and those we failed to support, and this weight can be overwhelming. The habit of postponement can result in lasting regret. This may manifest as delaying apologies, avoiding reconciliation, or neglecting communication with loved ones. It can also involve missing opportunities to spend time with family, pursue learning, or realise creative ambitions. When these dreams rely on our involvement, what are the consequences if we do not act? Do we allow guilt to persist, or can we extract meaningful lessons from these experiences?

*Jerusalem trip with in-laws, they had their
share of differences, but did some pilgrimages together*

We are learning to prioritise and fulfill small dreams, addressing those that can be realised without delay. By doing so, we experience the richness of life and nature. When a desire arises, we strive to fulfill it promptly. We encourage friends and family to embrace the present, as missed moments cannot be reclaimed. Living a fulfilling life requires intentional effort to address past postponements. While maintaining a bucket list is valuable, it is even more important to actively pursue and complete these aspirations. Let us strive to fulfill the dreams of our parents and loved ones, enriching our lives with meaningful experiences and minimising future regrets.

What is one small dream, what is the one small wish of yours or for someone you cherish, that you can begin to bring to life? Can you bring a smile on the face of a loved one? We just have an opportunity to start today, and the moment is now. Try to live rich and die poor!

If our unfulfilled dreams are the snapped lines of kites we let go too soon, our actions today are the hands that reach out to mend the fraying edges of our family's tapestry. We cannot go back to the snow of 2015 or to Delhi, but we can weave new patterns of presence today. By fulfilling the small wishes of those still with us, we ensure that when our own story is finally told, the fabric remains whole, the colours stay vibrant, and we leave behind a legacy rich in love and empty of regret.

CHAPTER 10
MY JOURNEY WITH JAYAKKA

My Leader and Friend - Vasanthmma

June 29th is a day I will never forget. It started like any other, but ended with a loss I can never replace. I remember telling Jayakka I would go home and come back the next day. She asked me to stay, her voice full of the same caring she always showed, especially to those she loved. Even though she wanted me to stay, I felt compelled to leave. Jen and Leebin were alone, and responsibilities at home weighed on me. After Akka's operation, as her health faded, Prabhakar, Prasad (my eldest nephew), and I tried to spend as much time with her as we could. It was painful to see her grow weaker, especially after knowing her for more than 64 years as someone so lively and easy going.

I would sit by her bed and watch her, my mind replaying scenes from our lives. Even after a stroke weakened her right hand and leg, she never lost heart, that was Jayakka. She met every challenge head-on with a mindset that inspired. I've never seen her buckle under stress or utter a word of surrender. Her grit to chase dreams was legendary. She was relentless, and our family never hindered her. I remember her visit to Auckland in 2015. She returned with many stories. One detail stuck with her, she was fascinated by how people in Auckland lived independently in their later years. She noticed that people aged eighty to ninety drove themselves, shopped in markets, lived alone, and led dignified lives, in sharp contrast to our culture. Jayakka questioned why we couldn't do the same, why we should always rely on our children. She returned to that topic often and tried, a few times, to live alone in the family home. Her belief in self-reliance and in shaping one's own destiny was unwavering.

Our conversations were always thoughtful and engaging. During the KGF days, when she came to Kolar for work and stayed overnight, those moments became special memories for me. We loved each other's company and would whisper late into the night so we wouldn't wake the children. Sundar Raj, my husband, used to joke that we were like "two schoolgirls with endless secrets," but he always respected how close we were. I didn't have many friends growing up, so Jayakka became my closest friend. We talked about everything. Our childhood, heartaches, joys, struggles, studies, and teachers. Later, we would talk about our children, their futures, and our own dreams. She was careful with money and always saved well. When she visited KGF, our shopping trips were quick because she knew what she wanted, which gave us more time to sit and talk over tea.

Time passed quickly, as it always does. The children grew up, and Akka's promotion took her work to Chikkaballapur. Our routine and our special late-night talks stopped for a few years. I felt a quiet pain from that absence, as if something important was missing from my daily life.

Later in my career, I moved to Chikkaballapur, allowing our lives to reconnect, though not with the same rhythm as before. Priorities had shifted, and relationships had matured. The reality differed from the idyllic image I had envisioned, yet our bond remained strong. The late-night conversations of KGF were replaced by more mature discussions as we faced new challenges and responsibilities. On June 29th, I planned to return home for a day or two to manage household matters, intending to come back and be with Akka.

I made sure everything was set at Akka's home, gave the nurse instructions, and left. I felt uneasy, as I often did when I had to leave because of other duties. After Sushma's accident and losing her, the hardest experience of my life, my attention turned completely to Jen (my grandson, Sushma's and Leebin's only child). Taking care of him became my main purpose, especially since he survived that tragedy. When I got home, I finished my chores and, feeling tired, went to sleep. I didn't know it would be the last time I'd see my sister, my leader, and my friend alive.

Duo Residency housewarming ceremony Dec 2004

I woke up suddenly when my phone rang. At first, I thought it was my alarm, but it was a call. The voice was unclear at first. I never expected that call, and I didn't understand the words right away. It was hard to take in. Akka had finished her journey here and was now with my Bava, her best friend. I didn't feel sadness, loss, sorrow, or even shock, I was lost, while I know she was seriously ill, I never thought I would lose her. Maybe after Sushma's accident, I couldn't feel shocked anymore. Still, it was very hard to accept that Akka was gone. As I learned what happened, I felt a wave of guilt. I kept thinking that if I had been there that night, maybe she wouldn't have passed away the next morning. It's a natural thought, and it keeps repeating in my mind, even though I know God has His own plan for each of us. With a heavy heart, I had to say goodbye to Jayakka. Everything happened so quickly that I couldn't fully understand what her absence meant.

A significant chapter of my life had concluded. By that time, all my elders had embarked on their final journey. Witnessing the departure of each older sibling since 1982 has been deeply sobering. It is never easy for the younger generation to lose every elder who came before them. The loss is particularly wrenching when the person is a friend, a leader, and a guide. Jayakka, who was both a mother and a role model to me, left a void that has been hard to reconcile.

Realising I had no one left to confide in, made the loss even harder. In the weeks and months after, I felt deeply lonely. I always talked to Jayakka without hesitation, but now life feels completely different, and I don't have anyone as close as she was. We were always there for each other, so I never knew this kind of emptiness before. I'm still trying to accept that I can't share everything with my sister anymore. In tough times, she was always the one I turned to for advice, comfort, or just to share little secrets. I try to move forward, hoping to be for someone else what my sister was for me. Her influence has been woven throughout my life, always present, a lasting part of my story from the very beginning.

My Early Years with Jayakka - by A S Prabhakar

My pillow holds secrets that only Jayakka (my elder sister), Vasanthakka (another elder sister), and I shared. I still remember those nights clearly. In our crowded home, we would huddle together, our heads on one pillow but facing different ways so we could talk privately. We whispered all night, talking about everything. These moments were special, no matter what we discussed, we always made decisions together before the night ended.

Our close bond didn't just happen by chance. It grew from the warmth of summer holidays when I was a child. I remember visiting Jayakka when she started her government job in Mandikal, a quiet village near Chikkaballapur. Prasad, Sudarshan, and I went everywhere with her. She never left us behind, instead, she included us in her work. I still remember the dust on our feet as we walked to villages that buses or cars couldn't reach. Even though we were much younger, she never saw us as a burden. She cared for us like a Mom. This was true for both my elder sisters, Ruthakka and Jayakka. Vasanthakka, who was only two years older than me, grew up right alongside me, and our lives were closely connected.

I spent a year living with Jayakka before starting my degree, a time that helped our relationship grow even stronger. I spent time with her and sometimes visited Daniel Bava, not knowing about their relationship. In 1969, Jayakka and Daniel Bava got married, and her love for life remained unchanged.

If I were to describe Jayakka in one word, it would be determination. Her ambitions extended beyond herself, as she aspired to improve life for the entire family. After only three years in her first job, she was selected for Health Visitor training. She relocated to Bangalore with her family to continue her education, while I pursued my graduation.

Our Aunt from Bangalore, Ruthamma and me

With help from our aunt, Mom's sister Ruthamma (in the picture above), who also worked in the Health Department, Jayakka finally got a posting in Bechaganahalli, after short assignments in Anekal and Bidadi. Our aunt didn't want Jayakka to go back to a village, since she, Bava, and Jayakka they had a great bond together. My aunt helped many of us move to Bangalore, giving us strength and guidance with both firmness and care. This showed how strong our family ties were, we were more than just relatives, we were each other's support. I still remember my first trip to Bangalore, which Jayakka arranged. We stayed at Divanarapalya, and with Bava and Akka, the city felt like a special gift they gave me.

Time passed swiftly. She transitioned into her new role, and I graduated. Since Akka and Jayanna's families resided in the same village, our visits were frequent and strengthened our bond. By the time Jayakka relocated to Gudibande, her home had become a shared space for all of us. There was no distinction between "mine" and "yours" and everything belonged to all of us. They welcomed every friend and family member warmly, creating a sense of belonging.

Despite being younger, I shared a strong rapport with them, allowing open discussions about family matters and personal challenges. They always respected my opinions and made me feel valued. When I married, Jayakka and Bava were my primary supporters, organising and blessing every aspect of the event with great affection.

After I married Linora and moved to Bangalore, life changed significantly. The city introduced new challenges and a period of uncertainty and self-reflection. Motivated by memories of past hardships, we were determined to achieve financial security and social respect. Although these struggles reduced the frequency of my meetings with Jayakka, the strength of our bond remained undiminished. We not only shared happy moments, but also had our fair share of misunderstandings and disagreements. But the respect we had for one another was a rock that never moved. Life moved too fast. We lost Bava at the young age of 57. It was a staggering jolt for Jayakka. I had seen how close they were, Bava being her pillar of strength and she his. Bava was a man of the people, and his friends loved Jayakka like a sister because of her dignity and kindness.

Jayakka was both authoritative and assertive, yet she always spoke thoughtfully. Her self-respect and her family's respect were paramount, she would do whatever was necessary to protect her loved ones. Once she placed her trust in someone, her loyalty was unwavering. Our wealth was not material, but was found in the love we shared. She was ambitious for us and showed the highest level of determination among all the siblings, which helped her achieve the goals she did.

I treasure the memories of our trips around Karnataka and especially our pilgrimage to Jerusalem. Even after her paralytic stroke limited her movement, her faith and commitment were amazing. She never complained.

When she eventually relocated to Bangalore, it felt like an echo of earlier times. Prasad was in Yelahanka, Vasanthakka was nearby, and Sudarshan frequently, so we were reunited. reunited. Even during her illness, Jayakka's primary concern was our well-being. In her final days, Vasanthakka and I spent hours by her bedside, engaged in conversation. The unspoken bond among us was palpable.

On June 29, 2017, at 10:30 p.m. I quietly said goodbye to Jayakka. Vasanthakka had just left. I told her son, Sharath, "Call me anytime if you need me." Even though I had visited every day for three months, I had never said that before. I don't know why I said that, that night.

At 5:00 a.m. the next day, the phone rang and a big chapter of my life ended. Jayakka had reached her final rest. I miss her every day. She was not just my sister, but also my inspiration, supporter, and the best friend a brother could have. Her absence has left a void that is not easy to fill, and I will live the rest of my life with the memories and strength she shared.

"Siblings are a gift from above."- A S Sudarshan

Childhood memories are lasting threads that shape who we are. They bring happiness, comfort, and teach us lessons that build our character. I was lucky to grow up in a home with six brothers and three sisters, there was always plenty of love.

As the youngest, I had a special place in the family. Dad and older brothers protected and provided for us. Even though money was tight, I never felt I was missing anything. I always felt safe. Mom was quiet and strict, but kind, and my father was gentle and encouraging. With my siblings, we built a world full of laughter and support. My brothers and sisters have always guided me.

Among these eight pillars of support, my second sister, lovingly called Jayakka, was always there for me. She was ten years older and cared for me with a kindness I still feel today.

One of our trips to interior karnataka

I'll never forget something from my early school days. Jayakka took part in the Independence Day celebrations as a Girl Guide. When she came home, she didn't talk about what she had done, but brought me a coconut sweet she had saved just for me. For a young boy, that was more than a treat, it was my first lesson in selflessness.

Jayakka was ahead of her time. As a visiting nurse in the 1980s, she traveled to remote villages near her headquarters. At a time when few women did, she learned to ride a scooter to travel far and wide, her work taking her to distant places at odd hours of the day. I still remember the villagers' amazement at seeing her, a true sign of her dedication. As we grew up, I remember the 18-kilometre trips from our hometown to visit her. She loved having us over, and her greatest joy was cooking, feeding us, and making everyone feel welcome. Those visits, along with our big family trips of 50–60 people, were always filled with laughter and gentle teasing that only a close family can share.

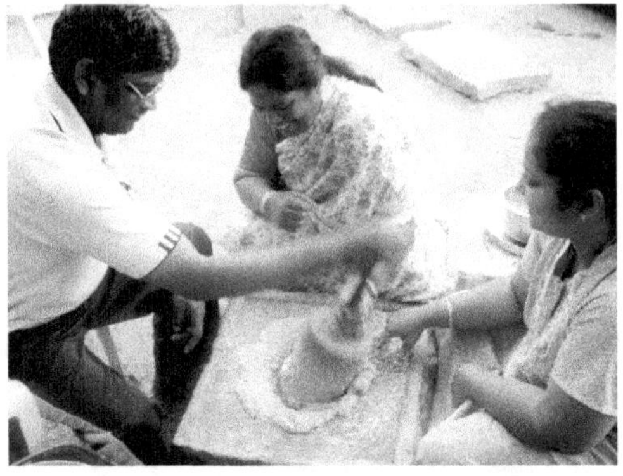

Me with Jayakka

The joint family system was more than just a way of living, it was the foundation of our culture. Even though Jayakka is no longer with us, her strength and kindness still live on in our family.

I am grateful to all my elders, but right now, my heart is with my dear sister Jayakka. Thank you for your love, your strength, and the life you shared with us.

As we lay our individual memories of Jayakka side by side, the coconut sweets, the late-night whispers, and the dust of the village roads, we see a portrait of a woman who was more than just a sister, she was the architect of our family's emotional safety. Whether she was leading us through the streets of Bangalore or riding her scooter through remote villages, she carried us all with her. Her life was the thread that pulled our separate journeys into a single, cohesive bond. Though her physical voice has fallen silent, the "Grit" she modeled and the "Grace" she gave so freely remain woven into the very fabric of our lives, ensuring that as long as we remember, we are never truly alone.

CHAPTER 11
THE RIPPLE EFFECT

To truly understand a life is to observe its impact on those it influenced. Mom's story, defined by dedication, courage, and faith, extended well beyond our home, generating a significant ripple effect in every community she became part of.

In the preceding chapters, you've seen her journey, the challenges she overcame, and the spirit she carried. Now, we turn the page to a different kind of testimony, a collection of voices that offer the most intimate portrait of her character. These are the friends, the extended family, and the individuals who were comforted, guided, or inspired by her simple presence.

It explores how she played a pivotal role in her extended family, forging bonds that transcended distance. It also examines her ability to profoundly impact others, particularly during their times of greatest need, while remaining unconcerned with judgment or consequence.

They highlight her willingness to stand firm when others hesitated, her open-mindedness that surpassed generational norms, and her consistent kindness. For many, she was the unwavering foundation and the beloved "Godmother," whose support was both active and deeply heartfelt.

A Tribute to My Chikkamma - By David Prasad S/o Ruthamma

I am the eldest nephew of my Chikkamma and the son of her eldest sibling, Ruthamma, who was the first among the nine siblings. As I reflect on our family history, I am eager to share my personal experiences and cherished memories of my aunt. Having retired as an 'A' Grade Football Coach from the Sports Authority of India, I have spent years observing people and leadership. Now, I want to recount the remarkable life I observed in her over the decades.

Our Chikkamma was a cultured, kind-hearted soul, a mother figure who loved everyone as if they were her own children.

While serving as an ANM (Auxiliary Nurse Midwife) in the Health Department in Mandikal, her responsibilities included daily visits to villages. She regularly inquired about the villagers' health and hygiene, offering guidance, advice, and instructions on health related matters. During my school holidays, I accompanied my aunt on these visits, which provided a unique and memorable experience. In every village, she was welcomed with respect and affection, and the residents diligently followed her health advice. We, as her family, also received special attention during these visits.

Mr. Daniel, my aunt's husband, served as a Post Master and was known for his kindness and discipline. While she was posted in Peresandra, they frequently invited the entire extended family, which included nine siblings and their children, to their home. We always appreciated their hospitality, and the time spent together remains memorable. They genuinely enjoyed hosting family gatherings, finding happiness in bringing everyone together. Notably, they consistently offered assistance to anyone in need, never refusing help or expressing hesitation.

They taught their children well regarding a disciplined life, dedicated work, and taking care of the family. They carried out their religious and civic duties in a way that was appreciated by society.

They were exemplary parents, with my Chikkamma demonstrating particular commitment to the family. She ensured that their children valued discipline, upheld cultural traditions, recognised the importance of education, and embraced values such as unity and generosity. As a result, my cousins Deepak, Sharath, and Sudheer received quality education, worked diligently, and now hold significant professional positions. Their achievements can be attributed to the guidance and example set by my Chikkamma and Chikkappa.

Education was of utmost importance to them. My Chikkamma not only encouraged others to pursue learning but also continued her own professional development by undertaking additional training, completing examinations, and obtaining certification. This enabled her to secure a prominent role in the district as the DNS (District Nursing Superintendent). She consistently led by example.

Following her retirement, Chikkamma relocated to Bangalore to reside with her children. She initially stayed with Deepak until his move to New Zealand, after which she lived with Sharath. The tradition of regular family visits continued, and she actively fostered unity by encouraging family gatherings and open communication. She was particularly adept at recognising and resolving conflicts among family members, always striving to maintain harmony. I deeply admired this aspect of her character.

Prasad with Mom

She valued and appreciated me for who I am, and I reciprocated her affection.

The Unwavering Heart of an Aunt - Arun Kumar S/o Sathyaraj

My aunt played a significant role in my life. As her nephew and the son of her third elder brother, I spent several holidays with my cousins at her home during both my childhood and teenage years. Although she maintained strict discipline, her kindness was even more pronounced. She ensured that all of us received the care and support necessary for our well-being and happiness.

Even during periods of familial difficulty, her love remained steadfast. She consistently supported and cared for me, demonstrating her unconditional affection. Her generosity and kindness were enduring influences in my life, and I remain deeply grateful for her presence. Her absence is profoundly felt.

The Iron Lady with a Heart of Gold - Leena Gladies D/o Jayaraju

With both sorrow and deep affection, I share these reflections about my soulmate, Athe (Maternal Aunt).

She was dynamic and energetic in all her endeavors. Professionally, she established an outstanding reputation through hard work and dedication. While she may have appeared unyielding to others, she possessed a deeply compassionate heart.

She consistently assisted others without seeking recognition, demonstrating quiet generosity and a willingness to help those in need. Although she was Dad's (Jayaraju) sister, our relationship extended far beyond familial ties. We shared a close bond, confiding in each other and supporting one another through various experiences. She was an "Iron Lady" who realised significant dreams, not only for herself but for the entire family.

She served as both a friend and a firm guide to her sons, shaping their development and character. Her dedication and unwavering support formed the foundation of their lives. She was the central pillar that unified our family.

Athe, your love and affection are boundless. Although time passes, our love for you endures. Your absence is deeply felt.

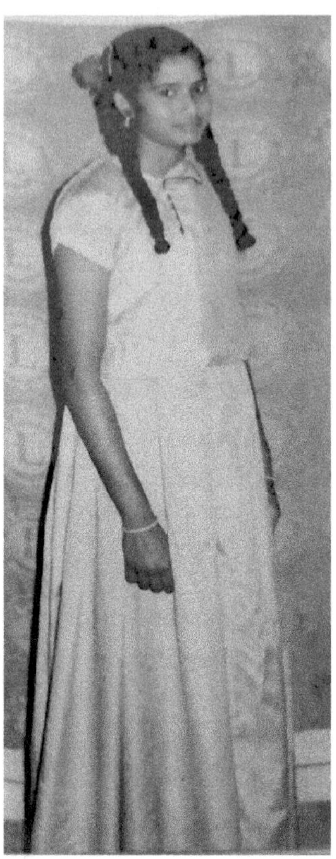

My photo taken at Gudibande Athe's place

Selfless Service, Unconditional Love - D. Sunil Dev Kumar S/o Devaraj

The first memory that comes to mind when I think of my aunt is her incredible selflessness. She was a true servant to the community, dedicating herself to the poor and needy in the most remote parts of Karnataka. I had the privilege of witnessing her compassionate work firsthand, as she would take me with her to visit villages during my school holidays. Those trips were my window into village life, and I saw a side of the world I'd never known.

Jayakka with Anoop and Grace

Our relationship was exceptionally close. She treated me as one of her own children, extending the same warmth and care without distinction. As the eldest of eleven cousins, I shared a unique connection with her and benefited from her special attention. She was a maternal figure to me, and her guidance was instrumental, including her significant involvement in my marriage to Grace.

Family was her highest priority. She was the most humble individual I have known, and her love established a lasting legacy.

Pioneering Spirit and Servant's Heart - Stanley Ebenezer S/o A S Prabhakar

Two qualities of Jaya Aunty remain especially memorable to me.

First, her unwavering dedication to serving others was evident at all times. Regardless of the hour or weather conditions, she responded to those seeking help, sometimes returning only the next day after assisting a patient. This steadfast commitment earned her profound admiration and respect in Perasandra, where she became a pillar of the community.

The other thing I always remember is her amazing courage and independence.

Aunty's family at my wedding.

She demonstrated remarkable courage by riding a scooter through the villages where she worked, a sight uncommon among her peers and unique within our extended family. Her willingness to do so reflected both her confidence and her progressive outlook. She was not only courageous but also ahead of her time.

Our Pillar of Strength - Sowmya & Joseph

Jaya Aunty was undoubtedly the foundation of our family. Her strength was a boundless resource, particularly for Prameela Mom. Following the loss of Ammamma (grandmother), Aunty provided unwavering and consistent support in every circumstance.

Aunty created a sacred space for Mom, a sanctuary of freedom and comfort where Mom knew she could speak about absolutely anything and everything. This openness was not reserved just for Amma, she was always completely open to deep discussions with me and Joseph (my husband), making us feel heard and valued.

Joseph, Sam and me

The Courage of Conviction

We saw the depth of her loyalty when Mom faced challenges in making crucial decisions, such as enrolling me in the nursing course. It was not a popular choice. It was a difficult situation, yet Aunty stood by Mom and me. Her support wasn't passive, it was active and powerful. She was right there, supporting Mom from the moment of the application until the final step of my admission. She gave Mom the strength to pursue what she knew was right for my future. (This reminds me of the story that I have heard that when Aunty joined her nursing school, she was very persistent and determined)

What truly set Aunty apart was her incredible, forward thinking spirit. When I was starting my graduation, she had a conversation with me that I will never forget. She told me to focus entirely on my studies for four years with no distractions. She also offered the most generous assurance,

"After you get a job, if you find anyone and ask me to get you married, I will arrange it, no matter the circumstances."

Such unconditional acceptance and broad mindedness were rare for her generation. Her approach reflected not only tolerance but also trust in my judgment and a willingness to offer unwavering support.

Aunty consistently demonstrated love and kindness towards both Mom and me. Her presence was a source of comfort and support that we will always cherish.

This love did not stop when I graduated and started working. God blessed me, and I found a great match for my life in Joseph, a God fearing, down to earth, and ambitious person. Aunty immediately extended her grace to our family. Joseph shared a great bond with Aunty, and his story beautifully illustrates her unconditional heart.

I (Joseph Krupa) want to share our memories of Jaya Aunty, someone who was so much more than an aunt to us. She was the one person who loved us without any fear. Her love and care for us was completely genuine and from the heart, and we can never forget the love she showered on Sowmya, Sam (our son), and me.

She consistently visited us, regardless of our location. She inquired about our financial situation and offered support during challenging times, always attentive to our well-being. She also demonstrated concern for Sam's future, encouraging prudent investments such as purchasing land or establishing a fixed deposit.

She was a significant source of encouragement for me, consistently supporting my ministry work and expressing genuine interest in my professional and spiritual development. In her final days, she requested my presence, engaging in conversation and asking me to pray for her children and their families.

She always told me I was her fourth son and that no matter what, I should stick by Somya. She often spoke to me about her life, reflecting on how God had been with her and our family through everything. She would encourage me by saying that God would always be with me, too. She even said that if I ever lacked support from any quarter, I shouldn't worry because she would be there to help us if we ever needed anything. She truly stayed true to her word and cared for us wholeheartedly.

I loved traveling with her. She would always ride in the front seat of the car with me, and we would have the best conversations. Sometimes I would tease her, and she would hit me playfully. She did not like being teased, but we always had such a happy time chatting. She was especially happy when I drove her to Ambavaram village near Gandikota, and she made sure to take a photo with the village nameboard.

Aunty's native village, which they had visited for the first time in 65 years.

Even in her final days, she requested prayers for family, expressing appreciation for my prayers. Upon her passing, I was deeply affected, recognising her irreplaceable role in my life due to the maternal love and care she provided.

Reflecting on the time spent with her is a cherished gift, allowing me to recall her love, care, and guidance.

The Compassionate Caregiver - Latha Pandi

Aunty was an exceptional caregiver, as evidenced by the care she provided to both me and my late husband, Anand. During periods of illness, she attended to us in her home with remarkable dedication. This experience remains unforgettable.

Ananda and Latha's marriage

Her compassionate nature extended to everyone, and she was an excellent caregiver for patients. If anyone arrived at her home with an ailment, she would immediately attend to their needs, regardless of her own activities. I learned much about patient care from her example.

I hold her in high regard, particularly for her independence. I recall witnessing her commute to work on a two wheeler, and I believe she was among the first women in the village to do so.

Aunty was consistently helpful, always the first to offer assistance when someone faced difficulties. She would readily respond, "I will give, I will do." Her care for everyone in the family was evident, and she maintained a polite and positive demeanor in all circumstances.

A Tribute to My Dear Chikkamma - Prameela W/o Samuel

After my marriage and relocation to Chikkaballapur, Chikkamma became my primary source of support. At that time, I was reserved, yet she consistently understood me. Her presence encouraged me to express myself more openly. Rather than imposing her advice, she offered gentle guidance, fostering my confidence and ensuring I never felt inadequate.

Her love and affection extended to my daughters, Smitha, Sweety, and Sowmya. Although she maintained high standards of discipline, she was always considerate of others' feelings. She cared for our family with nurturing warmth. Despite being significantly older and Mom's sister, she never misused her authority. She sincerely appreciated my cooking and frequently offered praise.

During periods of family misunderstanding or difficulty, she consistently supported me. Her strength was evident in her unwavering support for loved ones. On one occasion, when I found it challenging to communicate with a younger family member, Chikkamma intervened with such skill that the situation was resolved without conflict. She maintained honesty while safeguarding the dignity of others.

When my daughter Sowmya decided to pursue a BSc in Nursing, Chikkamma encouraged her to dream ambitiously and pursue her interests. She regularly inquired about Sowmya's progress. I consider myself fortunate that Mom and her sisters were so nurturing and supportive. Chikkamma assisted Sowmya during her BSc education.

with Chikkamma.

I recall with fondness how Chikkamma would travel from Peresandra or Gudibande to the hospital where she worked in Chikkaballapur. As the hospital was near my residence, she frequently visited us. Occasionally, she would take her Mom and me to afternoon cinema shows. I also valued our shopping trips together. When I later established a small saree business, she became my most dedicated customer, inviting me to her home and introducing me to her colleagues to help expand my business.

Over the years, we maintained a close relationship and visited each other frequently. She was my favorite aunt, and I held deep affection for her. Although I miss her daily, I continue to cherish the lessons she imparted.

The Embodiment of Parental Love and Guidance - BN Chanappa Reddy

Smt. A. S. Jayakka and Daniel Sir truly exemplify the principle, "Mother is God, Father is God" (Matru Devo Bhava, Pitru Devo Bhava).

I experienced a mothers affection (Vaatsalya) and a sister's love (Anuraga) in Jayakka. Jayakka and Daniel Sir took the place of my elder sister and elder brother, shaping my life.

Master (Daniel Sir) wholeheartedly embraced a decent, disciplined, and dignified life. It is his friendliness that made it possible for me to rise to this level today.

Jayakka is a mother figure (Matruswaroopi). The way she dedicated herself to service is a guiding light (Daarideepa) for many juniors, in her commitment to duty, she is truly unmatched.

In my life, where I do not have a mother or elder sister, she gave me the nectar of a mother's care (Akkare), a sister's love (Preeti), guidance (Margadarshana), and affection (Vaatsalya).

She is a great mother (Mahaamaate) who embraced me as one of her younger brothers and as a son among her children. She gave me love, trust, and guidance, and extended the love of an aunt (Sodarhatte Preeti) to my children, showering us with affection and maternal love (Mamate).

Her service in the Health Department is unforgettable (Avismaraneeya). Her commitment to duty and discipline serves as a model for many juniors. The manner in which she implemented programs and the effort she invested are truly commendable (Prashansaneeya).

Her social concern that even the last person in society should receive healthcare is praiseworthy. The incredible and wonderful way she worked day and night (Aharnishhi) with her staff during the eye camp organised in our Peresandra is magnificent (Amogha Adbhuta).

with my sister

I will never forget the support and help Jayakka and Master gave me in my personal life during my departmental training.

I am attached to this family because their children, Deepak (Babu), Sharath, and Sudheer, share the same emotions, affection, maternal love, and treat me as their own family.

I bless and pray that this family may always be blessed with happiness, peace, love, and trust. May they all live long, healthy, joyful, and peaceful lives.

As these voices coalesce, a singular image emerges of a woman who did not just inhabit a community, but actively strengthened its foundations. These tributes from nephews, nieces and friends prove that her "Grit" was not just a personal survival tool, but a shield she held up for others. Her "Grace" was not a passive trait, but an active, reaching love that turned cousins into sons and neighbours into family. She lived a life that was truly "rich," and in these shared memories, we find the currency of a legacy that will never be spent.

CHAPTER 12
GRACEFUL ACTS

Remembering a Life Full of Love - Sheeba W/o Sudheer

Aunty had an endearing habit that always made us smile. Whenever she wanted to call one of us, she would often run through several family members' names before reaching the correct one. By the time she got it right, we would both be laughing. These small moments truly reflected her unique character.

She found great joy in giving. She enjoyed making pickles and sharing them with everyone. Witnessing others appreciate what she had prepared brought her genuine happiness. When Mom was ill and we spent long, exhausting days at the hospital, Aunty would prepare lunch daily, especially the mudde and chutney that my father loved and brought it for us. She ensured we were nourished and cared for, even during challenging times. Her thoughtfulness was unwavering.

with Aunt at Hyderabad

She was our greatest supporter, consistently encouraging Sudheer and me to remain hopeful about starting our own family. She urged us to persist with our treatments and never lose hope, deeply wishing to see our family complete and happy.

Beyond her kindness, she had a creative and disciplined spirit. She loved drawing rough sketches and plans for construction, and she took immense pride in her home. She was always experimenting with new ways to clean, organise and decorate, keeping everything spotless and beautiful.

She also cherished coffee, not only for its taste but for the aroma that filled the house. She treasured the coffee maker she brought from Singapore. In retrospect, there is a poignant irony, as just before her diagnosis, she remarked, "I can't smell the coffee anymore." At the time, none of us realised the significance of this subtle change.

Hyderabad Golkonda

She was a woman of deep love and simple joys, and we miss her every day.

A Legacy of Faith and Grace - Smitha W/o Sharath

Jaya Aunty was more than a family member, she was a constant source of support, guidance, and nurturing love. With a sincere heart and hardworking spirit, she carried herself with quiet dignity that earned respect. Soft-spoken and peaceful, she brought calm and warmth into every room. We cherished the Saturdays and school vacations when her presence filled our homes with renewed joy and togetherness.

Ours is a big family, united by a commitment to care for one another throughout every stage of life. Even now, childhood memories remain vivid, and the desire to relive those days can be overwhelming.

I recall holidays at Jaya Aunty's house, enjoying walks along the riverbank and playing in the farmlands. Evenings were spent together on the terrace beneath the stars. Although cooking was not her main passion, her creativity flourished in other areas. She had a deep appreciation for gardening and flowers, and a natural talent for decorating, transforming her house into a sanctuary. Over the years, her appreciation for beauty was matched by her spiritual growth and deep faith.

Jaya Aunty's influence reached beyond our family. She dedicated her life to developing our family managed school, serving as a pillar of sincerity and commitment. She inspired parents, instilling confidence that their children could achieve a meaningful future. Her ambition, supported by her family, became a cornerstone of the town's educational foundation. The community continues to remember her for her unique combination of simplicity and dedication.

Jaya Aunty and Daniel Uncle were a testament to unity. Together, they were loved and respected by society, creating an environment where everyone felt safe, secure, and valued.

Her resilience was most evident when Daniel Uncle was hospitalised in a critical condition. While others might have lost hope, Jaya Aunty relied on her faith. She became stronger through prayer, facing each challenge with courage and deep trust in the Lord. Her boldness during the crisis remains one of her most admirable qualities.

The relationship between a mother-in-law and daughter-in-law is often complex, shaped by expectations and differing perspectives. When I joined the family, we encountered initial challenges, including communication struggles and the effort to empathise with each other's roles. Through the grace of God, we overcame these difficulties.

Over time, we developed a supportive bond that strengthened our relationship and enriched our family. I witnessed her unwavering positivity. Even after a sudden stroke that left her paralysed, she did not yield to helplessness. She accepted her new reality with resilience rooted in her faith in Jesus Christ.

Life contains both joy and sorrow, but the memories we leave behind endure. Jaya Aunty's life was remarkable in every sense. When she was diagnosed with a terminal illness, she did not allow her suffering to diminish her spirit. She faced the end bravely, guided by her spirituality and unwavering love for her family and friends until her final moments.

Our Creator led Jaya Aunty through her struggles, her victories, and her moments of quiet happiness. She has finished her race, and she has kept the faith.

May the Lord's peace be with her soul.

A Woman Ahead of Her Time - Asha W/o Deepak

My mother-in-law embodied both grit and grace, though she would not have described herself in those terms. She valued discipline, responsibility, and diligence. She managed her household with firm principles, guided by strong values and a deep sense of duty. In her world, order prevailed and everyone had a defined role.

When I married into the family, the early years were challenging. Like many intergenerational relationships, ours demanded patience and understanding. There were moments of friction that tested both our resolve. Gradually, we learned to understand each other, adjust expectations, and show acceptance. Beneath her firmness was a quiet grace, expressed through consistent, deliberate acts of care that held the family together.

She was, in many ways, ahead of her time. In her village, she rode a scooter, something few women dared to do, and perhaps she was one of the first women in her village or district. That simple act revealed her courage, her independence, her refusal to be limited by what was expected of her. For many years, she spent long hours away from home for work, carrying responsibilities that weighed heavily but never seemed to bend her. She did not complain. She did not seek recognition. She simply did what needed to be done. That was her grit, steady, unwavering, unspoken.

Her strength was most apparent after she suffered a stroke. Recovery was slow and challenging, but she approached it with the same determination that defined her life. She relearned to walk, speak, and manage daily tasks, facing each challenge without self-pity or complaint. Her persistence and grace enabled her to endure pain, setbacks, and the daily struggles of recovery with dignity, demonstrating that courage can be quiet and deeply personal.

Her stern exterior softened entirely with her grandson, Ben, whom she adored. With him, her love was unconditional and her warmth evident. She was gentle, attentive, and proud. Observing her with Ben revealed a tenderness and softness that complemented her strength.

I remember one night when Ben was little, refusing to sleep at two in the morning. I was exhausted, barely able to keep my eyes open, but she quietly took him and let him play with his toys until he finally drifted off. She never complained and never showed impatience, she simply cared, fully and quietly, letting him feel safe and loved in the small hours. On another occasion, when they quarrelled, it was like two kids fighting, both stubborn and testing boundaries. And yet, she handled it with care and patience, guiding him, teaching him values, showing him how to respect others and stand tall, even in disagreement. Those moments, tender and imperfect, revealed her deep love and the way she shaped the heart of our family.

New zealand

Her home reflected the same care she gave to life. Potted plants filled every corner, each nurtured with patience. She had a green thumb, understanding when to water and when to wait. The plants were more than decoration, symbolising her care, patience, and discipline. In many ways, they mirrored her life, nurtured through effort, sustained by discipline, and grown with both grit and grace.

In the final chapter of her life, illness arrived quietly and moved with frightening speed. By the time her kidney cancer was detected, it had already spread, bringing immense pain and daily struggle. Yet even then, she endured, bearing it with the same grit, dignity, and quiet determination with which she had borne life itself.

Surgery was recommended, presenting a difficult decision. She was understandably afraid, as surgery offered both hope and risk. I vividly remember our last conversation, when she asked if she should proceed. I assured her of her strength and resilience, qualities she had demonstrated throughout her life.

She underwent the operation but never fully recovered. The memory of our conversation, her fear, and the courage she displayed remains with me. She faced the end of her life just as she had faced every challenge, with perseverance, grit, and a grace revealed through steadfast endurance.

Her life was defined by responsibility, sacrifice, and quiet strength. She loved deeply, even if she did not always express it verbally. Her story is one of courage, evident not only in her work and her love for her family, but also in how she met her moments of fear with quiet strength.

Today, we remember her with gratitude and love, celebrating a life of resilience, independence, and purpose. Her grit formed our family's foundation, her grace softened it, and her love continues to influence every life she touches. Though her life ended sooner than we wished, her strength, love, and enduring spirit remain with us.

A Short Note about My Late Grandmother - Alan Grandson

My Grandmother remains one of the most powerful people in my life. She was a person whose love was shown through acts of care and concern to those who grew by her blessings. She had a way of her own, making a house feel like home. Although I was a small kid and cannot remember much, as far as I do remember, her care extended beyond routine. She had an extraordinary ability to make others feel safe. The values she lived by were living a simple lifestyle, showing respect to one another, and her unconditional love, all of these qualities she has shown have led me to become the person that I am today.

Jen, Sam, Me and Grandmom

Although I did not spend much time with my grandmother, the moments we shared were filled with joy, laughter, and peace. Her memory remains with me daily, not confined to a single period. Though she is no longer physically present, she lives on within us, reminding us that a truly caring person never leaves.

I hope she is proud of the person I have become. I wish she were here to guide me, but life is unpredictable. We must continue to grow into individuals she would be proud of.

I miss you, Grandma.

Remembering My Ajji - Ben Grandson

Some people are constants in life, quietly present and persistent. Ajji was that person for me, she was my rock. I know I often took her for granted as a child, not fully understanding the depth of her love. Now, I recognise her love as unconditional, constant, and steady. Her actions spoke more powerfully than words.

She just Was. She existed when I needed her most, often without me realising the depth of her presence in my life.

My parents worked long hours, but Ajji was always there to fill the gap. She raised me, cared for me, and loved me in ways I did not fully appreciate at that time. She was there when I woke up, when I came home, and when I needed comfort. I now realise just how much of my foundation was built on her love and care. Through all of her struggles, she remained strong. She never once wavered in her care for me, even when I did not show my appreciation.

I will never forget when she visited New Zealand. The cold and quiet landscape felt very different, new, and lonely compared to the warmth of back home. Like us, she had never experienced a climate like that before. I could tell that at first it was not easy for her, but despite the cold, she brought warmth with her. Her presence filled the room and made it feel alive again. Even in a place so different from home, she made it feel like home.

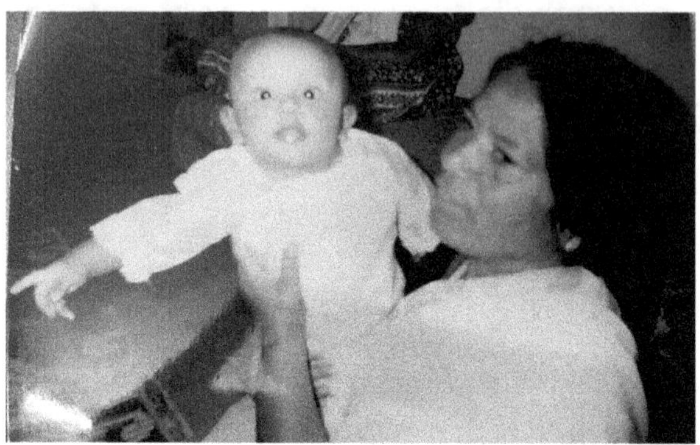

Me with Ajji when I was a tiny tot.

I now understand how profoundly she shaped me. I owe much of who I am to her. She taught me kindness, the importance of being present even in difficulty, and supporting loved ones regardless of distance or circumstance. Her lessons were simple yet profound, be kind to everyone, remain strong during challenges, and always strive to be your best self.

When I got the news of her passing, it felt like the world around me had shattered. I remember the day vividly. I was on the bus back home when I got a call from Mom. I did not know what was wrong at first until I got home. The news wounded me. I could not imagine my life without her. Even though we did not talk to each other every day, I could not accept that I would never be able to talk to her again.

Through my grief, I recognised that she was finally at peace, free from pain and suffering. After enduring her condition for so long, she deserved rest. I hope the love she showed me will continue to guide me in the years ahead.

With Ajji in New Zealand

Ajji was my strength, my mentor, and my heart. Her love lives in everything I do, every choice I make, and the person I strive to be. I will carry her warmth, her wisdom, and her love with me always.

The Golden Thread

Through the eyes of her daughters-in-law, we see a woman who reshaped our family, navigating the shifting tides of tradition and modernisation with quiet, indomitable strength. We see her riding her scooter into the wind, a "Quiet Revolutionary" who tended her garden with the same fierce discipline she applied to her soul.

Through her grandsons, we witness the most beautiful transformation, the "Godmother" softening into "Ajji." She became the steady rock in the center of their play, a silent presence that formed the foundation of their world. These stories remind us that a legacy is not carved in cold monuments, but is found in the warm aroma of morning coffee, the shared patience of a late-night story, and the quiet courage to face the final sunset with an unwavering faith.

Her journey has ended, but as these voices prove, her story is far from over. It lives on in the resilience of her sons, the grace of her daughters-in-law, and the bright, soaring futures of her grandchildren she so dearly loved. The lines of the kite are no longer snapped but held firmly in the hands of the next generation.

CHAPTER 13

MOM & ME

"Children grow best when their roots are free."
- Sudheer

As I reflect on my journey, I realise how deeply these words encapsulate my life's trajectory. Each courageous decision I made stems from a home where freedom was not merely spoken, but actively practiced. My upbringing prioritised experiential learning, supported by steadfast parental encouragement and a sincere respect for our individuality.

My bond with Mom is a treasure that grows stronger with time.

While many of my peers and elder brothers pursued engineering, I felt compelled to follow a different path. I was drawn to agriculture, motivated by a desire to contribute to food security. Initially uncertain about convincing my parents, given their preference for engineering, I expressed my true ambition. Although they were initially confused and suggested veterinary science, they ultimately recognised my passion and supported my decision wholeheartedly.

Commuting to university posed significant challenges. The public bus route was excessively time-consuming, and the available shortcut required a bicycle or motorbike. Financial constraints made purchasing a motorbike impossible, so I considered using an old, worn out bicycle. Instead, my parents made a deliberate sacrifice to buy a new Hercules MTB bicycle for my commute. I still possess that bicycle thirty-five years later. Their decision, though financially difficult, reflected their unwavering commitment to my education.

Upon securing my first job immediately after university, I vividly recall tears streaming down my parents' faces. These may have been tears of relief after years of dedication and hardship, or perhaps a profound sense of satisfaction. As the youngest in the family embarking on my career, I sensed their immense relief from the pressure they had endured to guide us towards personal growth.

My new job brought additional challenges for Mom. The research center was approximately 60 kilometers away, requiring me to leave home very early each morning. Mom would rise even earlier to prepare fresh food for my lunch box. Regardless of the season, she remained steadfast in her support. My parents' dedication ensured that I arrived at work on time. Even now, my brothers tease me about my work ethic, a trait I recognise as inherited from both parents. I take great pride when others note my determination mirrors Mom's.

During this period, I spent considerable time with my parents. Deepak had begun his career in Bangalore, while Sharath was occupied with contracts and completing his engineering degree. Mom encouraged me to assist with the agricultural work she led on our land. Convincing her that my academic research differed from our practical farming often became a source of humor. It evolved into a family joke, with all four of them playfully challenging me when I could not provide immediate solutions to the farm's daily issues.

After several months of work, I requested to purchase a motorcycle, specifically a Yamaha RX100, as my commute had become nearly unmanageable. Public transportation was limited, and at times, I travelled in the back of pickup vehicles. Recognising my difficulties, Dad secured a loan through his workplace to buy the motorcycle. This significantly eased my commute, reducing travel time from 2.5 hours to 1.5 hours. I found great joy in taking my parents for rides. Mom especially appreciated reliable vehicles, favoring the Bullet, the Yamaha, and her own scooter. Later, Sharath's Hero Honda became her preferred choice.

When our family established a school, Mom became fully engaged in its operations. While I assisted when needed, it was primarily Mom and Sharath, along with the dedicated support of Smitha and Sweety, who ensured the school's smooth functioning.

Later, when I shared my intention to marry Sheeba, both parents responded with sincere joy. They not only offered their blessing but also actively supported our union, celebrating our relationship wholeheartedly. Our journey together eventually brought us to Yelahanka, where we established our first home.

In November 2002, we endured a profound loss with Dad's passing, marking a significant period of transition. This was especially difficult for Mom, as Dad had been her source of strength for decades. Sheeba and I eventually moved to Attur to start our family in a new city. I deeply felt the absence of my parents' daily presence and made it a priority to visit Mom in Peresandra on weekends. During these visits, I shared my plans, challenges, and joys with her, which became a formative period of personal growth.

Eventually, I faced the difficult decision to relocate to Hyderabad for work. Although Mom was initially troubled by the distance, her love and support prevailed over her concerns. She understood that this move was essential for my personal and professional development.

Gandikotta Caves

During this period, our family was expanding its horizons. Sharath relocated to Bangalore, and Deepak prepared for his move to New Zealand. Although Mom knew she would remain alone in our hometown, she never discouraged us. She remained a steadfast and silent pillar of strength for each of us. Her visits to Hyderabad consistently brought warmth and joy. She particularly enjoyed the Charminar market, making it a priority to visit its vibrant lanes during every trip.

Life's path is rarely linear. In January 2014, I suffered a severe heart attack. My uncle Prabhakar intervened promptly, ensuring I reached the hospital in time. The news devastated Mom, who immediately rushed from Bangalore to Hyderabad and stayed with me for several months. Her presence provided immense comfort to both Sheeba and me. During her stay, she diligently managed all my medical needs and expressed deep concern for our wellbeing even suggesting I return to Bangalore, though circumstances prevented it at the time.

Her support was consistently empowering rather than passive. She respected our choices and offered guidance to help us navigate life's complexities. With remarkable dignity, she refrained from seeking financial involvement or exerting control over our lives. This trust extended to her daughters-in-law, whose education and careers she actively encouraged while honoring their individual parenting styles. Throughout her life, she valued trust and courage above control and fear. For her, life is caring and giving. While I escaped being an agricultural consultant for her, I couldn't stop myself from accompanying her to nurseries to get potted plants. The farm vehicle I used for commuting would often carry manure, pots, or plants on the way back home. She did not bother whose home it was. If she thought that she needed to get some plants and pots, I had to accompany her. Even Sharath and Deepak also had to do the same. She had decorated Peresandra house, Duo Residency and my house with plants. Even Sheeba is fond of plants and greenery so it worked out well for them. She was very happy to take care of and pet Scooby, our dog. I vividly remember that, as a child, I used to insist she bring the dogs home. While she liked them, it was too much for her to manage.

Charminar shopping @Hyderabad

Granting others the freedom to make independent decisions requires both generosity and confidence, as well as the ability to relinquish the fear of losing influence. This blend of freedom and foundational support was the greatest gift our parents offered. It is bittersweet to realise that the parents who instilled independence and courage in me, spent the least time with me during their final years. Just as we reached a stage where we longed to care for and cherish them, they embarked on their final journey.

My brothers and me, experienced fulfillment and success in both our personal and professional lives. Reflecting on the foundation of this achievement, I recognise that our parents empowered us to pursue our own paths and consistently supported us throughout our journeys. I continue to live by the cherished memories and enduring values they imparted.

A cherished Moment with Mom and Dad

I consider myself deeply fortunate to have had such parents. Their love granted us the freedom to pursue our ambitions while ensuring the security of a nurturing home.

Last Few Days with Mom

March 31st remains indelibly marked in my memory. On this day, Sharath conveyed the devastating news, Mom's PET scan results were unfavorable. The diagnosis was late stage cancer. In an instant, our world did not merely tremble, it collapsed.

The diagnosis of late stage cancer prompted a relentless surge of questions in our minds,

- Did we ignore the symptoms?
- Why didn't we get her checked earlier?
- How did the doctors miss this back in November?
- How much time do we have left?
- Why her?

We struggled with intense emotions, anger, confusion, helplessness, and a profound sense of failure. Each physician who had previously treated her seemed to represent an unfulfilled promise. In retrospect, I continue to believe that medical negligence occurred, as both subtle and critical signs were missed by us and overlooked by the professionals.

This sense of betrayal was intensified by memories of her character. In her prime, she was a dedicated healer who served rural women with exceptional commitment. She provided essential support to expectant mothers, remaining by their bedsides throughout the night and offering not only medical care but also genuine compassion. Her life was devoted to her principles, her patients, and the ideals of service.

> *"It remains a profound regret that, when she required care, the medical community did not demonstrate the same level of devotion she had consistently shown to others."*

As time passed, a persistent sense of guilt developed within me. I regretted being away from Bangalore and not being physically present as her circumstances worsened. This feeling continues to affect me. I believe I could have done more, acted with greater responsibility, and found additional time to spend with her. This regret will remain with me indefinitely. However, it has imparted an important lesson that, in future for any crisis, I must be present for those I love or love me. By doing so, I honor her kindness and, through compassionate actions, strive to embody the values she represented.

The Fight for Time

Following the diagnosis, we began an urgent search for the most effective hospitals, specialists, and potential treatments. We received advice from many sources. While some encouraged optimism, one colleague, who had lost his own sister to a similar illness, advised us to consider allowing nature to take its course.

However, we could not accept surrender. We wanted to explore all the options available. We chose to continue with the treatment, and after a successful surgery, we briefly allowed ourselves to hope for her recovery and return to normal.

During my visit to Bangalore in June

But her condition began to deteriorate. Hospital visits became more frequent, and witnessing her endure severe pain was deeply distressing. We felt powerless in the face of her suffering.

The Garden of Memories

Despite these challenges, some of my most cherished memories emerged during this period. At Sharath's home, I would accompany her downstairs in her wheelchair. We moved slowly through the parking area and paused near the garden, where her discomfort appeared to lessen. She would smell the flowers and discuss plant species, the chemistry of fragrances, and propagation techniques.

Our backyard garden in Peresandra was well known in the village as a sanctuary that Mom created herself. Today, this appreciation for nature continues among all of us. Both Deepak and I maintain gardens at our homes which are not merely hobbies but serve as living tributes to her passion. I am grateful that she witnessed us continuing her legacy during her lifetime.

180 Minutes

June 18th, 2017, remains a significant date in my memory. After lunch, I sat beside her and chatted and laughed, recalling past memories. As I massaged her hands and legs in an attempt to ease her discomfort, she gradually fell into a deep, peaceful sleep.

I observed her breathing, and this became one of my most cherished memories. She comforted me to sleep many times during my childhood. During the final days of her life, I carry a memory that I could relieve her pain and comfort her.

For the next two hours, I sat in silence, holding her hand and reflecting on numerous uncertainties,

- *Could a miracle still happen?*
- *Could we steal just a few more days?*
- *How can I make this better for her?*

Tears fell quietly as I sat in the stillness of the room. Those 180 minutes were among the most meaningful and emotional experiences of my life, shared between us.

That was the last time I spent time with her, those memories remain in me forever. I never got an opportunity again to take her for a walk near the garden. Whenever I pass that garden at Sharath's home her memory flashes back.

A Legacy of Action

Parents represent more than individuals as they are blessings whose significance is often fully realised only after their passing. Although I continue to feel the burden of not having done enough, I choose to transform this regret into a living tribute. We honor our parents not merely through words, but through our actions by demonstrating humility, kindness, and the same dedication to service that she exemplified.

Thank you, Mom, for being the constant light that guided us home.

- Your life is our inspiration.
- Your story is our strength.
- We will live up to your expectations.
- We will serve others as you served them.
- You were a blessing to the world, and we will endeavor to honor your legacy through our actions.

You were resourceful, selfless, and loved beyond measure.

Thank you and love you, Mom. Always.

A Life of Love and Devotion - Sharath

I have undergone significant personal transformation, particularly following the two most challenging periods at home in 2002 and 2017. Among the three brothers, I spent the most time residing with our parents, which allowed me to develop a deeper understanding of their personality. I was privileged to support them, caring for Dad during his illness and later for Mom.

It is so hard for me to pick just one moment or one story from my 40 plus years with them. To me, every single day was a new day. Every day, I learned something new about them, and every day, they helped me become a better person. Their life, the path they walked, their dreams, and the struggles they went through to reach them. It was nothing less than a grand saga.

Valued education over self

Throughout our lives, our parents had always emphasized the importance of education. This value became especially clear during a conversation I had with Mom. One day, seemingly out of nowhere, the topic of Alan's education came up. At the time, Alan was studying at our village school under the guidance of Mom and my wife, Smitha.

I suggested moving Alan to a top school in Bangalore. We had no plan when we talked about it. We hadn't discussed the details, what would happen to our own school, where we'd live, or how we'd manage. Mom was surprised. She always liked to plan and needed to understand everything before agreeing.

She had no clue how to respond because there was no preparation. Her first response was, "It is a great thought," but in her mind, she was wondering, "How is this possible?" My brothers, Deepak and Sudheer, were already settled in Bangalore, and the four of us were living in Peresandra. It was supposed to be a time for Mom to relax, manage the school, watch her grandkids, and travel.

This proposal was so unexpected. We had only built our home in Perasendra 13 years ago. We had gone through so much pain and so many challenges to build those memories, and we were just settling down. Now, I was suggesting a new "discrepancy" in our lives. But Mom was so supportive. After we talked it through, we finalised the move. We decided we would move to Bangalore to get Alan into Bishop Cotton Boys' School. When he got his seat there, we were all overjoyed. Our parents' dream for us had been passed down to me to do for our children. On the first day of school, Mom went with Alan. I remember how proud she looked seeing her grandson at Bishop Cotton Boys' school, something we never thought would happen. She was happier than any of us.

Bishop Cotton's Alan's first day of school

Mom's own struggle for education made it her highest priority. She had an opportunity to go for her DPHN training, a special one year course. She had actually postponed this for a few years because of our education and the house construction. When the final call came for the training, there was a lot of indecision at home. My brothers were already out of the house for work, and Mom did not want to leave Dad and me alone for a whole year.

It was such a hard decision. It was her chance for a promotion, but there were no guarantees. She was already

45, and she knew this was her last chance or she would miss the opportunity in her career. It was also a financial strain because she wouldn't be paid the full salary, that would be putting pressure on our normal living. I was so sad to see her prepare to travel to a place 550 kilometres away. I had not lived without my mom for many years, I was too attached to her. We couldn't talk or visit often, and it wasn't cheap to make visits to her training location. With a very heavy heart, she made the decision to go. Dad was her pillar and her strength, he always supported her, and even when they had their differences, they always found common ground. All our pain and hardship disappeared when we learnt she had passed the course with first class marks. Success always came to her because of her commitment and determination.

DPHN training Hostel

Never gave up on motivating and persuading me, as she was so committed in her own career, it was very hard for her to see me wanting to give up on my studies. I had a good start in Engineering, but I struggled and couldn't get through to my final year. I tried a few times and eventually decided I would just give up and do my construction business.

Mom could not digest this, she relentlessly encouraged, challenged and scolded me to continue my education. The only reason I kept trying was because of her encouragement. When we finally decided I would drop Engineering, she wasn't happy. She wanted her three sons to be equal in everything. One of her conditions was, "You must have a degree." So, I went to Tumkur to pursue my education and earned an Arts degree. It was the first time I ever stayed away from home, during the school time when I was admitted to St. Josephs Convent, and had to stay in my grandparents place, I did not stay there and against her will came back home and joined local school. Even after getting my arts degree, she didn't sit quietly, she entrusted me with my next assignment. She convinced me, she pushed me firmly and even screamed at me to finish my Engineering. I eventually did, and she was so happy to see her dream come true that all her boys had a good education.

The Strength of Her Care

Mom cared not only about education but also went the extra mile for everything the family needed. In her care, there were no slips or misses. After we got married, Dad suddenly fell ill and was bedridden for months. He had a stroke that made him immobile. This was not an easy time for Mom. She was close to a promotion, her workload was heavy, Dad needed constant care, and the school had to be managed.

With Mom during Goa Trip

She managed all four responsibilities flawlessly. One of my jobs was to help her when she gave Dad his sponge baths. I had to be there to support her. One morning, for some reason, I couldn't help her in her daily routine. It was not easy for her and she had to struggle to give him a bath. When people didn't do what they committed to, she would get very angry. I realised the impact of it, when she didn't speak to me for many days. It wasn't normal for me, it was a lesson for life to behave and commit and live through the expectations.

Because I always lived with her, we had an intellectual understanding. We didn't need to debate. We had our differences, but we agreed to disagree and moved on. She never complained. She never asked for things for herself. She even managed to enjoy the company of her daughter-in-law and, when arguments arose, made sure I was never pulled into it.

She had a special love for her siblings and her parents. No one could ever find fault with her family. She was always defensive of them. She gave us a great foundation on how to keep relationships alive and how to handle family conflicts with dignity.

With parents in Goa.

I have seen life through my parents' eyes. Today, I feel a profound sense of fulfilment to have been part of their lives. Mom and Dad are my pride. It is their blessing that makes us all happy today.

I feel her absence every day. The process of coping with her loss has been lengthy and difficult. My sole comfort lies in knowing that she is reunited with Dad, the love of her life.

Friend, Guide, and Philosopher - Deepak

I have always been a storyteller, and every story I tell, in some way, begins with Mom. There is one particular story I've carried with me since childhood, a tale told many times, of a family journeying through a great forest. It was a multi day journey and as food grew scarce, the Mom, without a word, would tear off a piece of her own bread and pass it into the small hands of her children. The Dad, a man of logic and reason, would mentally plot their next move, calculating distances and remaining rations. But one evening, a sudden roar shattered the stillness of the woods. A wild animal appeared before them, its eyes locked on the children. The man's mind raced, a whirlwind of tactical thought as he searched for a way to save his family. But the mother didn't hesitate. She moved on instinct, born of pure love. She leapt forward, meeting the beast head-on, her body a shield between it and her children.

Cape Reinga New Zealand

She was tired and exhausted, her body weakened from lack of food, living on nothing but water, yet her spirit was an unyielding force. She fought fiercely, not for herself, but for the safety of her children, for the future of her family. When the animal finally retreated, defeated, she was left bruised and weary, but she was unbroken. She gathered her children close, her silent strength a comfort. She worked with her husband to ensure they all reached the other side of the forest safely. I remember hearing this story as a child and feeling a simple joy that the family was safe. It was only as I grew older that I began to understand the deeper truth within the tale, the courage, the protection, the generosity, and the immense resilience a Mom embodies. The story was more than an adventure, it was a testament to the selfless love that holds a family together. Although Mom and I never traversed a literal forest, we navigated the complex and often unforgiving terrain of life together. The challenges we encountered, though invisible, were equally formidable and required resilience and mutual support, and we were ill equipped to solve them on our own.

Auckland museum table number and her age matched

Though I was the eldest, my time with Mom was often fragmented. From a young age, I was a boarder at various relatives' homes, living independently for my studies and early part of my career. This distance, coupled with the four and six year age gaps with my brothers, meant our bond was different. I wasn't close with my brothers as they were close to eachother, who were only a year and a half apart. The distance bred in me a habit of questioning everything. I was vocal, often acting as if my worldly experience made me more knowledgeable than my parents. In our teenage years, my brothers and I would often tell our parents that they didn't understand modern society. Our "big brains," swollen with a partial view of the world, didn't realise that it was they who had given us the foundation to see it at all.

I recall the irreverent manner in which we teased Dad, a respected leader who managed hundreds of staff. We joked that his military background, limited his perspective to absolutes, overlooking nuance. Despite his widespread friendships and the respect he commanded, neither he nor Mom responded negatively. Instead, they met our remarks with quiet amusement, reflecting a wisdom we did not yet appreciate. My upbringing among influential cousins in Chikkaballapur fostered a sense of fearlessness and, at times, arrogance. Mom often observed that my bond with immediate family was weaker than with extended relatives, a reflection I now recognise as accurate. I was like a kite soaring high, yet precariously tethered.

My true connection with Mom began much later, in the messy, challenging years of my early adulthood. My parents hailed from a world where formal education was a distant, shimmering dream. Both of my grandparents worked within the orbit of a mission run hospital, working as butlers and aides alongside British doctors and administrators. Growing up in those hallways, my parents observed the British with a sense of wonder, marvelling at the effortless grace of their English and watching their children pore over "big, big books" that seemed like sacred talismans of a different world. When Mom completed her 8th grade, the missionaries, recognising her sharp intellect, urged her to enter nurse training immediately. Yet my grandparents and Mom remained resolute in her determination that she would finish her 10th grade first. It was a bold stand, a testament to their collective foresight and her own quiet, burning ambition.

This fierce drive for education eventually paved my own path, though, ironically, it was the very thing that often pulled me away from the hearth of our home. My early years were spent under my grandparents' roof to attend St. Joseph's Convent, followed by two formative years in Tumkur to complete my 12th grade. By the time I returned home for my university years, the distance had settled in, and though we shared a roof, a true emotional bridge remained unbuilt.

The gap only widened after graduation. I entered a gruelling season of professional stagnation, unable to secure a steady job for 2 years. Driven by a mix of frustration and a need for independence, I moved out once more, drifting through a series of odd jobs and facing the cold realities of the world on my own. It was a time of searching and silence, a period where the "dots" of my life felt scattered and disconnected from the legacy my parents had worked so hard to build.

After Ben was born, I started to experience the very struggles Mom had likely navigated with mortgages, job insecurity, business failures, and the endless quest for perfection. My earlier life, before finishing my engineering degree, had been one of freedom, but Mom had always watched over me from afar. I recall those days in primary school when, once a month, I was given money to go to the movies with my friends, all on my own. My friend Krishna and I would go to a different city, a privilege I didn't appreciate then. While other families tagged their children with them, Mom gave me the freedom to explore the world.

Mom at home

She and Dad taught us practical life skills such as shopping in a vegetable market, bargaining for clothes, cooking, and respecting people. They taught us how to be a part of a community, how to dream, how to respect people, how to plan, how to help, what good is and most importantly, how not to disgrace the family name. Mom was very clear, it was zero tolerance for complaints. The moment a neighbour reported our bad behaviour, a family showdown would ensue. This constant exposure to a structured, disciplined environment prepared us for the challenges of adult life. While people today talk about mental health and suicidal tendencies, our parents had a different, perhaps more effective, approach to raising boys. It was easy for them, as we were three boys, and all the "discipline and punishment" began and ended with me. Sharath, the middle child, was the nice kid and received special care, and Sudheer, the youngest, got most of the love. This reminds me of another story, to control a whole village, you don't need to control every person in every house. You just need to control the most powerful one. I just cursed my luck, thinking I was being treated badly.

Mom's wisdom became clearer when I started raising Ben. When we were struggling, she knew exactly how to handle him. She told me countless times that I needed to be patient. She guided me on how to behave, how to navigate life's challenges. I was a carefree person then, but my wavelength was slowly beginning to align with hers. By 2007, I was fully listening to her guidance, though I still rebelled on some things, like her insistence on buying gold or land. I regret those decisions today.

Chickmangalur Trip

After we settled into our home in Bangalore, Mom joined us to assist with Ben, as both my wife and I were dedicated to our careers. When I faced job insecurity, I turned to her in distress. She responded with characteristic composure, "Big deal. What's the worst that can happen? You lose one job, and another will come. If not, don't worry, I will take care of you all." I lacked her confidence but as she predicted, the crisis passed. Although she appeared resilient, I now question whether she was as emotionally strong as she seemed. There were periods when she felt isolated, lacking support. After Dad's passing, she often reflected on his unwavering protection of her dignity, regardless of familial disputes. He was a gentleman, raised among women, who understood respect. In our youth, we failed to fully appreciate this.

A Connection Forged Over the Phone

My best moments with Mom were over the phone. For five to six years, while I was in Auckland, we spoke for at least an hour every day. If I didn't speak to her, it felt like something was missing. It was like talking to a friend, telling her everything. We would talk about everything and anything. Sometimes we fought, sometimes we teased each other. She had a very specific rule that she didn't like being teased or made fun of. She would give it back immediately. She was a friendly person, but it took time to become friends with her. Once you become her friend, she was fiercely loyal. In our new neighbourhood, she quickly got to know everyone. She had her walking group and kitty parties, and she was also a wonderful gardener. The mango, papaya, and curry leaves she planted in the layout now provide fruit for the entire community.

Mission Bay, New Zealand with her Coffee!

She had simple tastes in food. She loved mangoes, papayas, melons, oranges, pineapples, jackfruit, custard apples, and bananas. She loved corn and groundnuts (peanuts). She didn't like ragi mudde, but she loved upma, dosa, dal vada, and alu bonda. She was also a fan of spicy food, particularly chicken, fish, and all chutneys. She enjoyed Andhra-style meals as well as delicacies from Tamil Nadu and Kerala. She liked noodles, sometimes bread with butter and jam, and even oats porridge, though she hated rice porridge. She was a courageous cook, always experimenting, and she was very fast, though she didn't enjoy making sweets.

As a large family, we often went on trips and pilgrimages, where community cooking was a big part of our lives. Mom didn't thoroughly enjoy it, but she was never negative. Of all the places she travelled, she loved Velankanni, Goa, New Zealand, and Jerusalem the most. She and my doddamma (aunt) had introduced me to Velankanni, a pilgrimage we took many times. On one of those trips, Dad got diarrhoea and almost lost his life. The Frooti mango juice from Parle was a lifesaver.

Very curious, Geysers in Rotorua

These discussions with Mom, these shared moments, were my way of building character and learning how to negotiate life. When she passed, a massive void was created. It was a ritual, a daily routine, to speak with her, and I found it incredibly difficult to adjust to life without her. I had less time to talk to Dad, but with Mom, we spoke until the very end, even during the year she was in the hospital.

In her last ten years, her faith grew stronger. She began letting go of things that once bothered her. The courageous, determined, and challenging woman I knew became more matured, composed, and careful. She started saying "no" to things that hurt her. She was close to my aunt (Vasanthamma) and uncle (Prabhakar), and my cousin Prasad. She had a special affection for her brothers and was devastated when Samanna and Jayamama passed. The incident had a big impact on her well-being. This loss taught her that life is fragile. She began to live by a new rule, one she had seen in Dad, which was, "If you don't have anything to do, don't do it here." This drew her closer to her children, her grandchildren, and her faith.

Pramilamma and Radhamani,
Radhamani were Mom's best friends

The Legendary

Living without her is the hardest period of my life. When Dad passed, I didn't feel the loss as deeply, since Mom was still by our side. We all had just married, and we were in our own struggles with jobs and settling down, which conveniently helped us to divert our attention. But now, she is gone. I still see her in my dreams, and I am slowly trying to come to terms with life without her. I know I cannot change the shortcomings of the past, but I can live up to her guidance. It's easy to get carried away, but she is the one who keeps me rooted and sane.

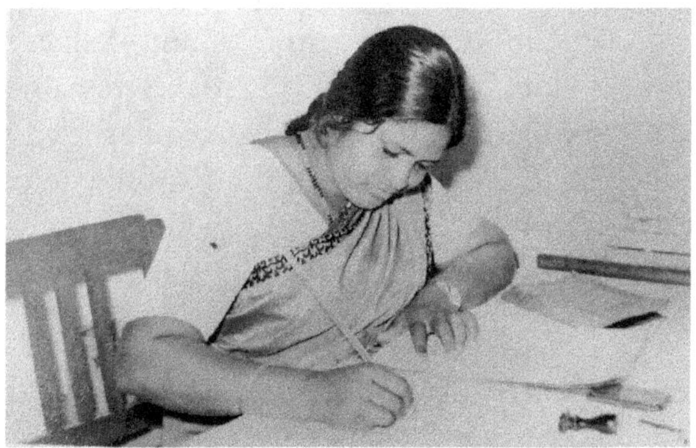

Mom's office

I try to live by the lessons she taught me, supporting and encourging the family as needed my brothers Sharath and Sudheer, supporting my sisters-in-law Smitha and Sheeba, and being the husband and father my wife Asha and sons Ben and Alan need. She gave us clear set of values to live by, and we are doing our best to honour her words. She wanted everyone in her life, but a few people were especially special to her, Sunil, Raju, Ananda, Leena, and Georgeanna.

Moms last picture with me

Within our culture, Moms serve as custodians of heritage, passing down traditions, customs, and values across generations. Mom exemplified this role. I remain deeply grateful for her kindness, love, guidance, and the gift of life. She taught me to view the world thoughtfully, to embody her ideals, and to lead a disciplined life. Each day, I reflect on the blessings she bestowed, which stand as a testament to her remarkable legacy.

Together, we carry different pieces of Mom's 'Grit and Grace.' Sudheer remembers her as the one who untied our wings, she gave us the freedom to find our own names and identities, refusing to let us be boxed in by tradition. Sharath saw her as our unshakeable anchor. Through the long winters of illness and the steep hills of our education, she was the fire that kept us moving, never allowing any of us to settle for a life smaller than our full potential.

As for me, she was my philosopher and guide. Our daily talks were the bridge we crossed together, moving from a simple mother-son bond into a deep, unshakable friendship.

Looking back, we see that her greatest masterpiece wasn't the school she built or the degrees she earned, it was the seeds of character she planted in us. She was our shield and our safety net, a steady hand that empowered us to chase the stars while always keeping our feet on the ground.

CHAPTER 14
LEADING THE LIFE SHE WANTED

In our family, we believe that true inheritance is not measured in wealth or property but in the values carried gently from one generation to the next. My two brothers and I were fortunate to receive these gifts from our parents and grandparents. Growing up in a close knit lower middle class community, where everyone knew and supported one another, we learned invaluable lessons about life and character from our family and our surroundings.

My parents maintained strict standards regarding our behaviour. They did not tolerate us speaking ill of anyone or causing disorder, either within or outside the home. Dad, a military man, was recognised for his discipline, honesty, and simplicity. Our parents balanced this structured environment with a sense of freedom and responsibility. They taught us right from wrong and the importance of respect, not through lectures, but through their actions. They demonstrated how to remain grounded, serve others, practice generosity, and respect the dignity of labor.

One of the most significant lessons we learned was Dad's unwavering commitment to equality. Having served on the nation's borders, he saw no distinction between the wealthy and the poor. We observed him treat people of all castes, classes, genders, and communities with equal respect and a spirit of service. Similarly, Mom, as a medical professional, provided every patient with equitable care, free from discrimination. While some may consider this as merely fulfilling professional obligations, my brothers and I recognised it as genuine service, extending beyond duty.

I am reminded of a story that truly exemplifies this. Mom once treated a patient from a very influential family, and the family members insisted that she follow a specific course of treatment. Mom, however, knew from her years of experience that their suggestion was not in the patient's best interest and could cause harm. Despite their threats and demands, she calmly but confidently stood her ground, explaining her medical reasoning and refusing to compromise the patient's health. Her courage to stand up to power and her confidence in her own professional knowledge taught us a profound lesson in ethical courage.

This value of equality is so ingrained in us that it once led to a misunderstanding at a family wedding. I was guarding the stage exit to the wedding reception stage to prevent a crowding the couple from the other side of the queue. When some "VIPs" tried to bypass the line and to go through exit route to wish the couple, I refused to let them go, valuing the people who had been patiently waiting in the queue. While this caused a family argument, it was a moment where I realised we were living the values our parents taught us, not through words, but through action.

Our parents demonstrated dedication through their own examples of hard work. Dad exhibited exceptional discipline, while Mom was deeply committed and industrious. Throughout their combined seventy years of professional experience, they never compromised their standards or neglected their responsibilities. This same sense of dedication and conscientiousness has been instilled in us, and we take pride in upholding it in our own careers.

Our parents also instilled in us a deep respect for elders. We observed them listening to their own parents without argument, even in disagreement. While Mom occasionally disciplined us physically when necessary, Dad relied solely on a stern look. When my brothers and I face significant decisions, we reflect on how our parents might have approached the situation and follow their way for resolution. Their guidance continues to influence us.

I often reflect on the truth that parents do not truly leave us, they live on through the values they etched into our character. There is a profound, quiet pride in seeing their legacy breathe through our own lives. Even today, being recognised simply as the "Postmaster's or Jayamakka's children" brings a swell of joy to my heart. It is more than a label, it is a North Star, confirming that we are walking the path they cleared for us. We have come to realise that while "it is very simple to be happy, it is very difficult to be simple." In a world of complexity, we find our greatest satisfaction in the same purposeful simplicity that defined them, a legacy not of things, but of being.

Reflecting on the past, I recognise that my book *Simplexity* emerged from the subtle, subconscious influence of my parents, whose lives inspired my personal transformation. This book serves as an invitation to live intentionally, guided by self defined values and a sense of fulfilling purpose. I maintain that gratitude is the ultimate guiding principle and the foundation of enduring success.

It highlights the transition from being children who were disciplined by an entire village to becoming men who discipline themselves according to their parents' standards. The book ends not just as a biography of Jayamma but as a manifesto for "Simplexity," the art of living a simple life in a complex world, guided by the ultimate principle of gratitude.

Grit and Grace

Reflecting on the mosaic of my parents' lives, I recognise that *Grit and Grace* serves as more than a biography of Mom, it offers a roadmap for living a meaningful life.

Within these pages, we have explored Dad's "mystery." Even now, I continue to uncover the depths of his quiet strength. Dad was unassuming and disciplined, never feeling compelled to justify dedication and demonstrating it through consistent action. He stands as evidence that one can embody both profound simplicity and remarkable strength. His grit provided the steady foundation for Mom's grace.

Through her resilience, Mom taught me a new approach to reasoning. She navigated life's most complex storms with binary clarity, allowing a simple "yes" or "no" to guide her decisions. Whether serving hundreds of villages in healthcare or facing stage four cancer, her spirit remained unwavering. She did not merely survive but evolved.

Together, they left an inheritance far surpassing material wealth. They imparted to us the philosophy of the "Full Soul"

- To Live Rich: Embody unconditional acceptance, pursue aspirations despite limited resources, and adopt simplicity as a guiding principle.
- To Die Poor: Conclude your journey having given every measure of your love, wisdom, and energy to others.

As you finish this book, I invite you to examine your own life through the lens of *Simplexity:*

- Are you living by principles you have defined, or by those imposed upon you?
- Today, tell it to the person who shaped you exactly what they mean to you. Do not wait for a "next time" that may never arrive.
- When confronted with adversity, remember the woman who served as a shield. That same strength lives within you.

Gratitude forms the foundation of all success. If these stories have inspired you, take the next step. Your legacy begins not tomorrow, but with the actions you choose today.

Compiled list of her favourites

Favourite Question	Mothers Favourite
Favourite breakfast	Akki Roti, Upma and Dosa
Favourite lunch	Mutton or Fish curry, Rice
Favourite dinner	Chapathi, Beans fry
Favourite snack	Lintel Vada, Chilli bajji, or Domurutu
Favourite dessert	Rice Payasam
Favourite street food	Bhel puri, Peanuts
Favourite restaurant	Shivaji, Kamath Restaurant
Favourite cuisine	Andhra style
Favourite fruit	Guava, Mango, Custard apple and Jackfruit
Favourite vegetable	Beetroot
Favourite hot beverage	Coffee
Favourite cold beverage	Grape juice
Favourite colour	Dark Maroon, Blue
Favourite colour to wear	White
Favourite outfit	Saree
Favourite footwear	Bata
Favourite accessory	Leather Handbag
Favourite fragrance	Jasmine
Favourite fragrance brand	Charlie
Favourite place in the world	New Zealand

Favourite holiday destination	Goa
Favourite city	Bangalore (Wanted to see Delhi)
Favourite travel memory	Singapore, Israel, New Zealand
Favourite weekend getaway	Chikkaballapur
Favourite time of the day	Morning
Favourite season	Rainy Season
Favourite way to relax	Lying on the couch and watching a movie
Favourite movie	Sharapanjara, Gejje Pooje, Halu Jeenu, Anthu leni katha, Jeevanatharangulu, Bandana
Favourite movie genre	Social
Favourite TV show	Antharangalu
Favourite musical Instrument	Harmonium/Keyboard
Favourite actor	Nageshwara Rao, Ananth Nag
Favourite actress	Saritha, Kalpana
Favourite song	Tamnam Tamnam Eradu Kanasu
Favourite music genre	Indian
Favourite singer	S. Janaki, S. P, Balasubramaniam

Favourite book	Marana Mrugandham, Abhilasaha
Favourite author	Triveni, Yandamoori Veerendranath, Yaddanapudi Sulochana Rani
Favourite fictional character	Phantom
Favourite sport	Cricket (because of family)
Favourite sportsperson	P.T. Usha, Kapil Dev
Favourite physical activity	Walking
Favourite indoor game	Carrom board
Favourite hobby	Gardening and Reading
Favourite weekend activity	Going to Church and sleeping in the afternoon
Favourite way to spend free time	Chatting with family and reading
Favourite gadget	Radio Transistor
Favourite subject	Medical Sciences
Favourite skill	Diagnosing the problem
Favourite work task	Presenting and Public Speaking
Favourite person	Indira Gandhi, Ramkrishna Hegde
Favourite teacher	Head Madam

Favourite mentor	Jayanna
Favourite friend	Radhamani
Favourite memory	CSI Compound
Favourite life lesson	Taking loan with high interest
Favourite achievement	Own Home, Settled Children
Favourite childhood moment	Time spent with brothers and sisters
Favourite compliment	"Your kids are great"
Favourite personal quality	Determination and Commitment
Favourite festival	Easter
Favourite celebration	Christmas
Favourite smell	Smell of the first rain on dry soil
Favourite weather	Spring
Favourite belief	God will take care of her
Favourite way to start the day	Coffee and listening to spiritual songs
Favourite Time spent	Spending time with Alan and Ben

Favourite car	Tata Sierra
Favourite bike	Hero Honda
Favourite vehicle brand	Honda
Favourite road trip	Velankeni & Hyderabad
Favourite mode of transport	Train journey and travelling by car
Favourite watch	HMT and Titan
Favourite book you own	Bible
Favourite personal possession	Diamond set
Favourite luxury item	Diamond Set
Favourite son	Sudheer
Favourite Nephew	George, Sunil and Ananda
Favourite Niece	Leena and Meena
Favourite sister	Elder sister Ruthamma
Favourite brother	Jaya Mama
Favourite aunt	Dodda Ruthakka (Mom's sister)
Favourite parent	Dad
Favourite boss	Dr. Anwarjan
Favourite person to talk to	Sister Vasanthamma
Favourite house	God's Grace, Daniel's Cottage

Favourite Family Friend	Channapa and Anand Murthy families
Favourite job role	LHV (Lady Health Visitor)
Favourite workplace	Gudibande Hospital
Favourite project	House construction (any)
Favourite achievement at work	Becoming DNS (District Nursing Superintendent)
Favourite indulgence	Arun Ice Cream
Favourite mantra	Help
Favourite life philosophy	Simplicity
Favourite family value to pass on	Living with loved ones
Non-favourite turning point in life	Husband's demise when life was looking good
Favourite risk taken	Home construction with very little money
Favourite failure	Attempting to be an agriculturist/ farmer
Favourite success	Children's stability
Favourite spiritual practice	Communion Services
Favourite place of peace	St. Mary's Basilica, Bangalore
Favourite Spiritual Song	Vijaya raja neene
Favourite Flower	Jasmine and Kanakambara

www.ingramcontent.com/pod-product-compliance
Lightning Source LLC
Chambersburg PA
CBHW061438050726
47593CB00006B/2392